CROSSING THE BRIDGE TO
Animal Consciousness

ANIMAL SOULOLOGY

ANNIE BOURKE

ANNIE BOURKE

CROSSING THE BRIDGE TO
Animal Consciousness

ANIMAL SOULOLOGY

DISCLAIMER

All the information, techniques, skills and concepts contained within this publication are of the nature of general comment only and are not in any way recommended as individual advice. The intent is to offer a variety of information to provide a wider range of choices now and in the future, recognising that we all have widely diverse circumstances and viewpoints. Should any reader choose to make use of the information contained herein, this is their decision, and the contributors (and their companies), authors and publishers do not assume any responsibilities whatsoever under any condition or circumstances. It is recommended that the reader obtain their own independent advice.

First Edition 2023
Second Edition 2025

Copyright © 2025 Anne Bourke

All rights are reserved. The material contained within this book is protected by copyright law, no part may be copied, reproduced, presented, stored, communicated or transmitted in any form by any means without prior written permission.

National Library of Australia
Cataloguing-in-Publication entry:

Crossing the Bridge to Animal Consciousness: Animal Soulology - Annie Bourke 2nd ed.

ISBN: 978-1-923197-60-2 (paperback)
       978-1-923197-61-9 (eBook)

A catalogue record for this book is available from the National Library of Australia

Published by Putting Words Publishing
www.puttingwords.com

For further information about orders: email CHIntuitive@bigpond.com
Photo credits: Front cover "Naoise" by Zoo Studio
                  Back cover "Tiernay and Annie" by Sumico Photography

DEDICATION

To my cats, who have shared their wisdom so that I can share it with you.

Thank you for expanding my consciousness.

To every animal who has had a conversation with me.

Thank you for helping me understand the importance of animals on a deeper level.

"When I look into the eyes of an animal
I do not see an animal.
I see a living being.
I see a friend.
I feel a soul."

ANTHONY DOUGLAS WILLIAMS

"Until one has loved an animal,
a part of one's soul remains
unawakened."

ANATOLE FRANCE

CONTENTS

Dedication		
"Animals" poem		2
Introduction		3
Chapter 1	Animal soul reincarnation	7
Chapter 2	Animal soul journeys	17
Chapter 3	Soul connections	35
Chapter 4	Preparing for goodbye	45
Chapter 5	Dealing with animal bereavement and grief	49
Chapter 6	Animals' perspectives on reincarnation	75
Chapter 7	Welcoming your animal home	79
Chapter 8	Eternal soul existence	97
Chapter 9	Soul secrets	99
Chapter 10	Issues with reconnecting	107
Chapter 11	Multiple dimensionality and simultaneous lifetimes	111
Chapter 12	Dying to come back	115
Chapter 13	Reality revealed	143
Acknowledgements		151
Connect with Annie		153
About Annie		155
Resources		157

ANIMALS
A POEM BY ANNIE POON © 2023

Many animals we have all known, but we understand none of them we own
They simply agree to accompany us on our earthly journey
Some, like ourselves, temporarily in physicality, others purely in spirit only
Or, there can be a combining and entwining
Of the physical and metaphysical in love unconditional

A light and bright essence of presence like the feline energy
Which does accompany me on life's journey
On padded paws, with sharp claws
Soft strokable fur, a comforting purr
Back strong, tail generally long
Whiskers that twitch and eyes that bewitch
Cats we know playfully sow seeds of love in our heart
And although our feline friends may physically depart
We can still hear the purr which does stir the vein of love which does remain

The feline energy continues to playfully accompany us on our journey
Along with, certainly for me, the equine energy.
Hooves clopping, Tails swishing, Warm breath huffing, and snorting, haunting whinnying
All signs of beloved equines present, in spirit

And of course as well as horse spirits and cat spirits, there are the canines
Happy loving whines, a bark, a yap, ears that flap
Toenails scrabbling, tails waggling, and we suppose the feel of a cold wet nose
A lick, a nip, a nuzzle from a friendly muzzle
We incline to believe in each sign of the canine, the equine, the feline, the bovine, the ovine, the porcine, or ursine and any other 'ine'
Or animal spirit which holds true on our pathway, guiding us, loving us in their special way
They all have the art of stirring our heart.
They lend their strength our whole life's length and beyond.

INTRODUCTION

From my cat Naoise:

"The seen and the unseen.

Galactic guardians, guidance, and inconceivable truths.

Permutations of wisdom discovered and rediscovered through the ages.

The stars, the celestial map, galaxies and crystal knowledge all contributing to your total transformation.

Animals understand and can teach you about timeless wonders and the mysteries of millennia.

Now is the time!

You are ready to understand, integrate and expand the perceptions of impossible to current reality.

This will involve a total paradigm shift, a leap of faith and a quantum change of knowledge and perspectives. This will promote thinking and challenging your preconceived ideas and your current understanding of why you are here and here now.

This is guaranteed to make you deeply conscious of the hitherto unknown and make sense of the inexplicable.

There have been energetic beings in existence for longer than you currently have proof of.

Many of the advanced technologies developed and finessed through ancient civilizations arose from interactions and knowledge experienced with wise ones. Some animals have had human and animal experiences in these times and know so much more than you do in modern times - and they are here to help you.

Inwards is the place to start. The reality of everyday chaos around you makes finding and following the spiritual path challenging. When you can meditate and achieve a space and place of calm, you can open up to hearing guidance, activating dormant wisdom, gaining clarity about what you are here to do and how to do it."

Telepathic communication is how animals communicate with each other. It is silent – you can't hear it with your ears. I consider it the language of love. Humans can learn to master telepathic communication and have conversations with animals living or in spirit, which is what I do. I also mentor animal parents so that they can communicate telepathically with their own animals. It is strange adjusting to it at first. You hear their voices in your head, not audibly in your ears. Animals have different voices, accents and tones just like humans. You can tell when they are smiling, some are practical jokers, some evoke powerful emotions with their words and experiences, and I've had a horse unexpectedly sing some of her answers. Telepathic communication includes verbal messages, visual messages (letters of words, images or video snippets) and sharing of emotions and feelings.

Introduction

The information I share in this book is based on the telepathic conversations I have had with many animals, some of whose stories you'll read. Telepathic communication is a profound and effective way to connect with your animals on a deeper level and understand more about them, yourself and the mysteries of life.

Spending quiet time with your animals is necessary when you have animals in your lives as teachers. Often they have waited patiently for you to wake up and recognise that they are here to help you. When I finally realised that my cat Reilly was here to be my teacher and acknowledged this, she said, "About time!" It must be so frustrating for them, waiting for you to be ready when they have so much wisdom to share, but they don't complain. Once you have woken up to your spiritual being and started exploring your spiritual purpose, animals can help you to achieve change and transformation.

We have this inner knowing that there is a greater purpose to being and unravelling this mystery takes time. We get told that our purpose, our 'why?' is linked to our passion but sometimes this can seem hidden. What is it that fills your heart with joy, has you floating in a stream of bliss, energises you and fulfils you?

Animals can teach you so much about your purpose, your past lives, your soul connections, ancient wisdom to thrive and can reveal the reality of life.

May the wisdom animals have shared with me open your hearts, minds and souls to the awe and miracles of life, and life after life.

CHAPTER 1

Animal Soul Reincarnation

CHAPTER 1
Animal Soul Reincarnation

I had no knowledge that animal souls could reincarnate till I experienced it firsthand. I had always been fascinated with how the ancient Egyptians knew about reincarnation and the extensive preparations that they made for the next life. I'd never read anything about animals reincarnating so this whole experience has really opened my eyes to the reality of soul journeys.

Reilly

CHAPTER 1: Animal soul reincarnation

My cat Reilly was one of my original animal communication teachers and she was amazingly accurate with the information that she shared with me. She expanded my knowledge on many topics including healing and crystals.

One morning I looked at her and for some reason I felt that her colour was a bit grey even though she didn't have grey fur. I asked her if she was okay and she didn't respond as she was having an earnest conversation with her brother cat so I went to the kitchen to get their breakfast ready. I heard this horrific screaming and I couldn't imagine what was happening. I raced back to her and she was just screaming but I couldn't see what was wrong so I thought I'd better take her to the vet and find out what was causing her so much distress. I quickly put on my shoes and when I went to pick her up she'd passed away. A few moments ago she had been alive and now I had a limp, lifeless cat. This was just an absolute shock because she wasn't very old and she had no health issues. I was saying "No, no, no, no, no." I didn't want to believe that she had gone. I had no idea what had happened or why she had suddenly left me. I took her to the vet and they confirmed that she had passed away with the diagnosis of a heart attack. She had never had heart issues or any circulatory problems.

I didn't know how long I'd have to wait to connect with her soul on the other side. At least I was in the unique position where I knew I would be able to have a mediumship conversation with her when she was ready and find out what had happened and why. Fortunately I was able to speak with her on the day that she passed which was very helpful because I had to know whether she wanted to be cremated or buried. Since she was the first cat that I'd ever been communicating with to be in the position to ask this question, I didn't know how she would answer.

She told me that she wanted to be cremated and she had very particular requirements for her funeral urn. She requested a brass urn with a particular shade of blue which was significant for her, and silver. When I spoke with a staff member at the animal crematorium the only blue urns they had were pottery, with a gold rim, so not what she wanted. I explained that Reilly had requested a particular urn, and the staff member said she had seen something like that on eBay. I had never bought anything from eBay and felt wary about buying a potentially pre-used urn so I searched online for animal funeral urns. I found a business in Melbourne called Furry Souls which had only started a month earlier. On their page of brass urns I found an urn hand-painted with enamel in the correct shade of blue with an inlay of nickel flowers. The urn was called Forget-me-not. It was exactly what Reilly wanted and she knew I would find it.

She was sending me a message "MI, MI" and I thought she was trying to tell me about a crystal, then received the message that MI meant myocardial infarct, and she was confirming that she'd had a heart attack. She asked to have pink tourmaline crystals in her urn. When I looked at the crystal's properties I found that they support the heart and assist with heart attack recovery. It was her way of confirming that it was definitely her that I was talking with as she knew so much about crystals and their healing benefits.

I asked her why she had passed away and my actual words were "What did you do that for?" I was still in a state of shock and totally surprised by the unexpectedness of her earlier than anticipated

CHAPTER 1: Animal soul reincarnation

departure. She said in a very matter of fact tone, "Oh, I needed a new body," as though that's what everybody did. I was swirling in a state of confusion trying to process what she told me. I was thinking "What?" I had no idea what she was talking about and it just sounded so unbelievable. Then she told me, "Stop being so sentimental. I'm coming back." This was something I was not expecting but interestingly she'd spoken to her cat brothers about what she was doing. They weren't pining and they weren't off their food. I was the one who was upset. They knew what she'd planned and they knew that she was coming back. They told me, "It's a temporary reprieve till she's back to boss us around again."

I had to trust that Reilly was telling me the truth because she had been so accurate with everything that she had been teaching me. I know a lot of people thought it was some weird grief coping technique to imagine that your animal was going to come back to you but Reilly taught me to trust and have faith. She described what she was going to look like in her new kitten body.

I did have a very strong feeling on a full moon that Reilly had reincarnated and had been conceived as a kitten and was back in the physical plane. Sure enough two months later she was born and I was able to go and meet her at six weeks old after she'd had her first lot of vaccinations. I must admit that there are no words to truly describe the unbelievable feelings of joy, euphoria and relief blended with the incredibly surreal situation of reconnecting with your animal again. It is just phenomenal to experience animal soul reincarnation and it was so exciting to hold Reilly in my arms again as 'Naoise' (pronounced Neesha - she picked the Celtic name which means Warrioress). I had to wait till she was about three months old before I could bring her home and having her home also was very surreal because she knew where everything in the house was. Within a couple of days it was as though she'd never left us. She was lounging on her brothers using them as pillows and cheekily trying to steal their food. I've since described the experience to people saying it feels as though they've just been away on a holiday where they've had a full body makeover and are home again.

Naoise

Although Reilly (now as Naoise) has a different tortoiseshell coat pattern this time, her colours are similar. Interestingly it's her unique behaviours and, as I spell it, 'purrsonality', that are so alike to last time. She still doesn't like strangers. She still prefers having time on her own away from everyone else. She loved sitting on the

CHAPTER 1: Animal soul reincarnation

back of my recliner chair grooming my hair and that's where she started sitting as soon as she came home – it's her space and her place.

When your animals incarnate they have a life purpose and soul lessons to learn just like we do as souls experiencing a human lifetime. In her previous life as Reilly she was very independent and seemed aloof which is unusual for the breed whereas her brother cat Paddy was an absolute lap cat and radiated unconditional love. I worked out during that relationship with Reilly that she was here to learn how to accept love - how to receive it and how to show love. I used to keep telling her that I loved her and I just wanted her to be able to accept that genuine love from me and hoped that she could share her love with me. Before she passed she was able to do that which was wonderful because that was what she was here to learn. Now that she's back as a higher evolved version of herself she's mastered that lesson and takes great delight in being very affectionate with me and kissing me. It's as though she's saying, "You know I learned my lesson last time. I know exactly what I'm supposed to be doing." It is so incredible that animals can master their soul lessons and remember them in their next lifetime.

I now recognise that Reilly deliberately chose to pass away at that time because she knew that there was the opportunity to come back in the new kitten body. It meant she could spend more time with me in the physical realm supporting me and my life purpose. She could have stayed in spirit and continued to teach me, but witnessing her return and understanding the immensity of animal soul reincarnation was such a powerful lesson for me. She also knew that I could write about my experience and help other animal parents who are grieving the loss of their animals. Her legacy means that I've been able to help so many bereaved animal parents because when I have a conversation with an animal in spirit I can ask if they know if they're going to reincarnate in this lifetime. Some of them know just before they pass away and sometimes they know just after they've passed away if there's a body available for them to reincarnate in. Occasionally we have to wait a long time for them to come back but it's definitely worth the wait.

The whole emotional rollercoaster journey with losing Reilly and welcoming Naoise has totally changed my understanding of soul journeys. I know irrefutably that life does not end when a human or animal passes away. Although the physical body no longer exists, the soul endures forever. We can always contact our animals, we can always connect with them and many of them do come back.

Reilly started this whole chain of realisation for me, teaching me what happens beyond life. It is the most incredible fact that I have learned from my conversations with animals. It has made such a difference knowing that animals can reunite with their families. I'm very grateful to Reilly and Naoise for helping me to experience and understand the miracle of reincarnation. Soul reincarnation is just so awe-inspiring and mind boggling. I've had to totally rethink my understanding of reality and embrace and accept the concept that there is life after life.

To expand my consciousness, Reilly and Naoise continue to teach me so that I can share their wisdom once I comprehend it. I talk with Reilly in spirit and I talk with Naoise in the physical realm, the latter having a higher evolved aspect of Reilly's soul in her. They've taught me that when they do reincarnate it's an aspect of their soul that comes back so they aren't the same. It's a higher evolved aspect of the former soul because the soul has been learning lessons during their former lifetime and mastering those lessons helps to evolve the soul. When they reincarnate they come back with a new life purpose and new soul lessons to learn. I've had to adjust to speaking to two aspects of the same soul when I talk with Reilly and Naoise – they have different voices. I'm used to it now but it was certainly strange trying to logically process and get my head around what I was being taught.

I now know that animal soul reincarnation is not just an occasional occurrence. I've had many clients whose animals have come back to them. I think it's incredible that our animals are so committed to their humans that they find ways to come back to us and be with us for another lifetime. There are powerful soul connections and soul contracts in effect for our animals to support us and deepen our relationships through lifetimes together.

CHAPTER 2

Animal Soul Journeys

CHAPTER 2
Animal Soul Journeys

Through gaining a greater understanding of your animals you can transform your relationships with them.

There are three key messages animals consider essential for you to know as animal parents:

1. Animals understand everything that you say. They choose how they respond. They can decide if they want to obey your requests or not as they have free will, but they certainly hear what you tell them. If you don't want them doing something, such as jumping on a table, instead of saying, "Don't do that," explain why you don't want them to do that. They can consider your rationale in their decision-making process. I spoke with a Mum recently whose cat was delighting in climbing curtains despite being asked not to. I suggested Mum explain why she didn't want her curtains being climbed. She explained her reasons to the cat and the cat stopped climbing the curtains.

From working with animals in my Animal Communication Mentorship Program, I am aware of the extensive vocabularies animals have. They know so much more than "no" and "walk." Some of the words they know are not commonly used in modern conversations. I feel that these animals have had past lives and are familiar with words and phrases from the eras they lived in. They have used words in the exercises we practise that their parents and I

CHAPTER 2: Animal soul journeys

have never heard of, but when I check in the dictionary, the words are there.

My cat Lileas has been working with one of my clients who does not have domestic animals to practise telepathic communication with at present. In one of the activities, my client had to send Lileas a verbal word telepathically and then ask her to send back verbally the word she received. My client sent the word 'transform.' Lileas sent back the word 'transmogrify.' To my knowledge I've never used that word so she hasn't learnt it from me. When checking the dictionary I discovered it means to transform in an unexpected or magical way. She received the word accurately and sent another word with the same meaning demonstrating that she understood but also showing that she could express herself in a unique way.

Animals are also sensitive to the frequency of words. If you use positive language, they will respond and be empowered. The simplest way to start changing your relationship with your animal is to tell them verbally that you love them and are grateful that they are in your life. Instinctively they do know that you love them, but hearing you verbally using the high frequency words "love" and "grateful" uplifts them on an energetic level. Since you never know how long your animals are going to be with you, it's a good habit to not take their presence for granted, and tell them every day how you feel about them. I've had so many people tell me how much this has affected the closeness of their interactions just by adding this one simple action daily.

Since animals are so aware of the frequencies and meanings of words, what you call them as a name or nickname is very important. Calling them unflattering or ambiguous names can be a psychologically negative experience for them. If you need to talk about something negative, try to do it out of hearing range of your animals. Becoming more sensitive and considerate of your language can make a significant difference for your animals.

2. Animals are very intelligent and very intuitive – they know what is going on with you. They are very sensitive to vibrational frequencies and changes so can detect your vibrational frequency drop when you become unwell. They often know before you are consciously aware that you are ill. They are also very attuned to your emotional status, like walking mood barometers – they know if you are sad or upset. If you are becoming unwell or are not your normal self, they will instinctively spend more time with you, sometimes beside you or on you to help with the healing process and help support your emotional wellbeing.

Your animals understand you on many levels. There is no illusion and you can't hide anything. They see the real you. There is no judgement or criticism, only unconditional love. They want what is for your highest good and can provide constructive advice for you. They know your past and they know your future and the next steps to take.

3. They are in your life for a reason – there is no coincidence that they are with you. They may have a soul connection with you and have had past lives with you in this lifetime

or previous lifetimes and have deliberately come back to continue supporting you. They may be with you to assist with your life purpose and soul lessons or with you so that you can help them with theirs. Sometimes animals are here to learn about receiving love and giving love and rely on you to help them master this lesson.

They also take on key roles to support you. Some animal souls are with you as guardians and are very protective of you and diligent with guarding your property and alerting you to possible danger. Some are healers and particularly come to work with humans who do energetic healing work to enhance and amplify what they do. My cats understand the frequencies and healing properties of crystals. They help to activate and energise the crystal grids I make to support the health and wellbeing of animals and humans. Some animals are teachers, and are with you to share wisdom and help you on your spiritual path. Once you can communicate with them telepathically they can start guiding you as you progress on your soul evolution and ascension path.

Each time a soul incarnates on Earth (either as an animal or human) there is a specific purpose for being here and specific soul lessons to learn. These change with each lifetime. Souls keep experiencing the same situations until they can master the soul lessons. My understanding is that, as souls, we have a choice about incarnating as a human or an animal. For those of you interested in astrology, in your human charts linked to the place, time and planetary alignments at your birth there is information about your life purpose, lessons and animals. You can also look at your animals' astrology charts and learn about their life purpose and soul lessons. It's another way to understand more about why your souls are together and how you are helping one another.

Animals have shared that when they pass over, they integrate the lessons that they have mastered which is an integral part of soul evolution. If it is an animal's destiny to reincarnate and return to their humans, it is a higher evolved aspect of their soul that returns in a new body, so they are not exact replicas. Sometimes they can look almost identical and have very similar mannerisms and sometimes they are very different – different species, different breed, different gender and different colour. Despite their outer appearance, at a soul and heart level you will recognise them and know who they are, and they recognise you.

In my mediumship conversations with animals in spirit, when they know that they are definitely reincarnating, they can tell me the relevant information about breed, gender and colour, and sometimes a time frame so that I can advise their human parents and they can prepare for welcoming them home. Knowing that your precious animal's soul is going to reincarnate powerfully affects the grief process. Yes you do miss their physical presence as they are no longer in your home giving you comfort, unconditional love, companionship and more. They make such a huge impact on your life and it hurts so much when they leave because you love them so much. Once you know that they are going to reincarnate there is an overwhelming sense of anticipation and excitement to see what they will look like, what behaviours you recognise and what you feel when you see them and hold them for the first time

CHAPTER 2: Animal soul journeys

in their new physical body. Not all animals reincarnate, so when you get to experience this phenomenon, it is a true gift being able to have another lifetime of love and connection with a beautiful soul you know.

Squintz's story

Squintz

Squintz is a beautiful cat in spirit who had been a blind rescue cat. He passed away in tragic circumstances and his Mum had lots of questions for him. He was very happy to answer the questions and acutely aware of the guilt his Mum was still feeling years afterwards. He wanted her to release those stored and unnecessary emotions. He knew that what happened with his passing was not her fault, and he did not blame her.

Part way through our conversation I heard the word "Rumpleteaser." I'd never seen or heard that word before. I did wonder if Squintz meant Rumpelstiltskin, but that made no sense with the context of our conversation. It's easy to doubt what you are hearing in telepathic animal communication and I assumed I was just hearing things, so I ignored it.

As we continued our conversation he said, "Rumpleteaser" again, very clearly. I knew then that I wasn't mishearing, and that I needed to pass this message on to his Mum. I sent her a message and asked if he'd ever been called Rumpleteaser – it was an intuitive feeling. Mum didn't respond for a while so I started to think that she might be thinking that I was crazy!

Then I received her response: "Oh yes, I'd forgotten that." She explained that when she rescued Squintz he was living with a dog called Rumple. He would get into trouble for teasing the dog, so got called Rumpleteaser. He was blind and couldn't even see the dog!

How clever of Squintz to send this particular word to me. There's no rational explanation for how that word got into my head apart from him telling me. It confirmed beyond a doubt for his Mum that I was definitely talking with her cat in spirit.

This experience was very profound and helped me to understand that animals in spirit could send a word which I now refer to as a 'code word.' The word makes no sense to me and has no relevance to our conversation but means something significant for their human parent. I'm in awe that they can do this, and it has happened during conversations with other animals in spirit.

CHAPTER 2: Animal soul journeys

For the parents, receiving the code word provides that extra reassurance and proof that their animal's soul continues to exist and that they are contactable through animal mediumship (communication with animals in spirit). This can effectively relieve the burden of stress, anxiety, guilt, remorse and regret which may have been present for years. Getting answers to questions can provide so much peace of mind.

During our conversation, Squintz revealed that he would reincarnate. My hairs literally stood on end when Mum posted a story about a stray male ginger cat she had rescued who has a significant eye injury. The synchronicities are no coincidence.

Key wisdom:

- Your animals in spirit know you are grieving and that you can hold so many different emotions about their passing. Storing emotions long term can affect your health and your animals want you to be healthy and happy.

- Animals want their humans to know that they have transitioned to the other side and that they are safe. Sending a 'code word' is such a clever method of assuring their humans that their soul endures and that connection with them is achievable.

I had a conversation with a cat in spirit who had passed away suddenly and traumatically. During the conversation he said the word "Penny." I asked him to explain. He said, "Pennies from Heaven." He wouldn't tell me anything else so I wasn't sure if he was referring to the poem or the movie and hoped his Mum would be able to decipher his message. This message was deeply significant. Penny is Mum's dog in spirit. I had no idea Mum had a dog, let alone known the dog's name. The message was actually "Penny's from Heaven" which the cat knew his Mum would understand. Animals' ingenuity in passing on uniquely specific and distinct messages to their humans and confirming their ongoing existence is just phenomenal. You may be sceptical, but there is no way I can just pluck such meaningful words and names out of the air. It's what the animals want me to hear so that their humans receive their messages and are comforted by the genuine connection.

Geisha's story

Geisha

CHAPTER 2: Animal soul journeys

This is a wonderful example of a strong soul connection between animal and human, and having resilience and faith to overcome obstacles.

I met Mum when she wanted me to have a conversation with her beloved cat Geisha in spirit. Mum wanted to know if Geisha was going to reincarnate in Mum's lifetime, and if so, what kind of animal she would be.

Geisha said she was definitely coming back, but Mum would have to wait a few months. She told me she was coming back as a Scottie dog (terrier), that she would be male, and the colour wheaten (white). She requested to be called 'Peyton' (and not the alternative spelling Payton), which means 'Royal.' She also reassured Mum that in the interim she would continue to visit her energetically as she had been, and said she would continue to visit even after she returns as Peyton.

I was intrigued that she was so adamant about coming back as a dog. She said she wanted "holiday adventures with the whole family. I don't like being left behind."

She also told me, "Tomatoes." I asked her to elaborate and she said, "No, it's a test." I wondered if she wanted to eat tomatoes as a dog, so I searched online to see if it is safe for dogs to eat tomatoes. The safety advice I found stated that as long as there are no stems, flowers or leaves, small quantities of ripe red tomatoes are safe for dogs to eat.

What really surprised and amazed me was that on the web page with this information was a photo of a Scottie dog with a bowl of tomatoes. This was totally unexpected and sounds bizarre, but I interpreted this as a confirmation sign of Geisha reincarnating as a terrier as she had told me. There's no rational explanation for seeing this image of the exact same dog breed just after she gave me the terrier and tomatoes messages.

When I told Mum about the tomato story and the terrier picture on the web page she said, "Oh Annie, tomatoes are my favourite food - I eat them every day and Geisha knows this." This was Geisha's code word for her Mum, proving that I was talking with her.

Mum duly started searching for available male wheaten coloured terriers. She found one and was counting down the days to bring him home, when the situation changed with the puppy no longer available. Mum said she felt like she was losing Geisha all over again.

I spoke with Geisha who told me that she was working on another option and to leave it to her to sort out. When I spoke with her again, she had found another wheaten male terrier for her soul to swap into. Mum sent me a photo of the puppy when she found him, and I was able to confirm that an aspect of Geisha's soul was in the puppy body.

Peyton

After getting everything ready at home for a puppy, with new toys and a fenced in yard, Peyton's humans welcomed him home. He knew his human parents, knew where everything in the house was, and settled back very quickly. He has played with some of his cat toys as well as his new dog toys.

He immediately bonded with his humans as though he had never left. I was fascinated to see how Geisha would adjust to being in a dog body after being a cat. Mum reported that Peyton can do everything that Geisha did, apart from being able to leap onto the bed at night to kiss his humans goodnight and sleep. He has been supplied with a set of steps so he can continue his bedtime rituals.

Peyton has relished going on walks, visiting dog friendly cafes, interacting with people and being admired. He has been on holidays away with the family and thrived with the experiences. The soul connection and bonds of love are undeniable. Peyton's parents recognise so much of Geisha in his actions and behaviour. They know their Geisha is home.

Key wisdom:

- Every animal I've spoken with who is reincarnating wants a new name. Sometimes they have selected their preferred name and sometimes they are happy for their human to choose. They are aware that if they look similar to last time that they are likely to be called by their former name through habit some of the time and they are not concerned about that.

- Even when they find a physical body to swap into so that they can reincarnate, sometimes circumstances change and the body is no longer available. In situations where this has happened, the animals have been able to find another physical body to return in. Sometimes this means that there is a further delay with their return, but they do everything they can to return to their humans as soon as possible.

- It's amazing that although the reincarnating soul is in a new body, they retain their memory of their past life and are familiar with their family members, the layout of their home and know where the food and toys are. It seems to take a couple of days for your other animals to accept them. It's such reassuring confirmation of who they are when they play with their former favourite toys.

- With soul reincarnation, an aspect of the soul comes to Earth in a different body and an aspect of the soul stays on the other side. Geisha can choose to visit energetically at any time even though an aspect of her is now present physically in Peyton. Mum can be comforted by having ongoing connections with both of them.

- I often get asked if animals reincarnate as the same species. In most cases the cats I have spoken with in spirit come back as cats, but sometimes as a different breed. I've had the same experience with dogs coming back as dogs and it's been so fascinating learning about so many different breeds of dogs and cross breeds so that I can provide the families with accurate information of who to look for. There are exceptions to this, and Geisha's reincarnation is one. She taught me that souls do have some choice in the body they come back in. She was determined to return as a dog, and she has.

CHAPTER 2: Animal soul journeys

Tigerlily's story

Tigerlily

Tigerlily is a much loved cat who passed away in tragic circumstances. (I deliberately use present tense as her soul exists and will exist for eternity). Mum had intuitively felt she was a reincarnation of a former cat, which Tigerlily confirmed. Tigerlily also let me know that she was going to reincarnate again in this lifetime.

Although Tigerlily and her fur sister Layla shared a relationship where love wasn't always shown to be equally reciprocated, Layla adored her sister. When Tigerlily came back for energetic visits after her passing, Layla would stare at her even though Mum couldn't see her. She often appeared when Mum was consoling Layla, and her presence frightened Layla to start with till she understood it was her sister's energetic frequency that she was experiencing.

Mum was eager to know when Tigerlily was going to return and what she would look like. Tigerlily said that she was going to be born within two months and would be home by August. She said she would be a male lilac coloured Tonkinese cat. I had to do some research to check Tonkinese fur colours and was relieved to see lilac in the list. She also requested to be called 'Harry.' I scrolled through online pages of Tonkinese kittens and they looked adorable. Mum did some research to find out more about the Tonkinese breed. She told me that the Tonkinese cats are a mix of Siamese and Burmese cats. She shared that the first version of Tigerlily is a Siamese, and Tigerlily is a Burmese cross, so how special to have a blend of both in Harry highlighting the successive soul connections.

I was asked to ask Tigerlily why she left so suddenly. She explained that she knew she had an opportunity to come back and spend longer with Mum, so she took that chance. She said, "I know it was sudden, and I've had to adjust too, but it will all be worth it when I'm home." She apologised for causing her Mum stress and sadness. She said, "I want her to know I'm okay and I want her to be okay."

She shared that she had found her life lessons challenging as Tigerlily. She said that as Harry her lessons would be "to love others (and commented that Layla would be surprised with this), accepting boundaries instead of pushing them, and being fulfilled and content with what is around me." She recognised that she would "have a different personality next time so won't be so challenging and demanding. I'll lap up being worshipped." She said, "As a pedigree cat I will need to stay inside and be pampered!"

After a lot of searching, Mum found a breeder with a large lilac male kitten. When I tuned into the photo of the very young kitten, I received the message that Tigerlily's soul had not yet entered the kitten, but had confirmation that this was the kitten whose body she was going to reincarnate in. Tigerlily was very excited that Mum had found her.

When Mum sent me a photo of the kitten when he was six weeks old, I knew that Tigerlily's soul was in him.

Harry

Harry arrived home in August just as Tigerlily had told us. Harry loves his Mum and enjoys smothering Layla with love. He is showing so many of Tigerlily's naughty behaviours but Mum knows he is irresistible, purring and gazing into his Mum's eyes. Love is eternal.

Key wisdom:

- When animals come back for an energetic visit, although humans can't sense them, you can hear, see, smell or feel them. Your living animals are very sensitive to energetic frequencies so they will sense when an animal in spirit visits, and will look fixedly at something that you can't see.

- As humans, when we incarnate, we go through what is termed "the veil of amnesia" and we seem to forget our past lives, and what our new soul purpose and soul lessons are. Animals as pure beings have the ability to remember their past lives and know what their purpose and lessons are in the current lifetime.

- Some animal souls wait till their human parents have found the body that they are going to reincarnate in before their soul swaps in.

- Your animals are just as excited to be coming back as you are.

CHAPTER 3

Soul Connections

CHAPTER 3
Soul Connections

One of the amazing facts that animals can help you to understand is that they may have soul connections with you. They may have had lifetimes with you previously. This may be lifetimes in your current lifetime such as a childhood pet who has reincarnated back to you. I've spoken with people who have thought there was something familiar about their animal but they didn't know why and they weren't aware that soul reincarnation could happen. I've also spoken with a lot of animals who have told me that they've had past lifetimes with their humans and this may have been as an animal or a human. To me it's so interesting that most humans have no memories of their past lives (unless they have flashbacks or past life regression sessions) but animals can recall their past lives, explain how you were connected and tell you some of the details about your history with them.

I spoke with one animal who told me that they had a lifetime with their human in 1919 in Houston, Texas. Now I wasn't sure whether Houston had actually been established by then but when I did the research I discovered it had been. Your animal may have been a different animal with you in a past lifetime and they may not have been a domestic animal.

CHAPTER 3: Soul connections

Sirius

I recently had a conversation with Sirius. He showed me through video, images, and verbal messages that he had been a pink and black pig with his human Dad in mid-west America in the 1800s. When I researched this information, the mid-west opened up in the 1800s, and pig farming was one of the agricultural practices. Dad told me that his parents in this lifetime had pigs. The synchronicity is unfathomable.

Your animal may have had human lifetimes with you, so they may have been your child, parent or grandparent or they may have been someone that you were very close to akin to family. To me it is absolutely fascinating discovering these soul connections through time and appreciating why we feel such a close bond with our animals.

Inanna (L) and Ishtar

Inanna and Ishtar are beautiful sister cats now in spirit who lived into their 20s and passed within a year of each other. Mum is very intuitive and was curious about past life connections, and wanted to know if they have any plans to reincarnate.

When I spoke with Inanna, she confirmed that she and her sister had had previous lifetimes together and also separate connections with Mum. Inanna shared that she had a human lifetime as a Roman centurion in Turkey and her Mum was in a role like a lieutenant, and was her brother. She also had a human lifetime in Ancient Greece as a poet and Mum was her (human) female muse.

CHAPTER 3: Soul connections

In the early 1900s in America, Inanna was an Appaloosa horse, and Ishtar was a draft horse and Mum was their male owner. The girls also had a lifetime as Mum's human daughters near Dartmoor in the United Kingdom in the 1750's. Mum told me afterwards that she was aware of a past life in the south of England where her husband was a sailor.

I am so impressed that animals can readily recall their past lives and provide so much detail. I'm so intrigued with what they tell me and research everything to see that the timelines and events are accurate historically - and they always are.

Their conversations about reincarnation were positive. Inanna told me, "I'm coming back – I know she's keen to know that. It will be when she has the time and space. At this stage Ishtar and I are considering Corgis, a female and male. It will be wonderful to come back together and be reunited with Mum but we have to wait a little longer. I can't wait!" When I spoke with Ishtar she said, "Yes we will reincarnate together. While Mum has Yoda (a male cat who walks on a lead) we would like to explore being dogs. Mum will be able to walk us all although perhaps not together but that would be fun. We'd like to come back into brother and sister bodies, and continue our close bond. We think Mum will be ready for us in 1-2 years. Whatever form we come back in, we are coming back together. Mum can tell us when she's getting closer to being ready so we can negotiate our return."

They obviously know it's their destiny to reincarnate and know they have some choice as to which bodies they reincarnate in. They also know that the circumstances aren't right for them to return at the moment and they are happy to wait till they can be reunited with Mum and their fur brother.

Paddy

I know from my conversations with my cat Paddy that we had a lifetime together in ancient Egypt a couple of thousand years ago. He told me that he was an Abyssinian cat and that I was a priestess working in the Great Pyramid. He actually showed me video snippets of our life together at that time. He also told me that he has had human lifetimes with me as well as animal lifetimes. He has been a cat with me in this lifetime as one of my original animal communication teachers and he's now reincarnated in this lifetime. I understand that our souls have kept connecting over thousands of years, weaving through animal and human lifetimes together.

I've since learned that when we have an unbelievably close bond with an animal and we don't understand why it's such a close connection that these tend to be souls who we've had multiple lifetimes with. There is a genuinely strong soul connection with the souls in some of our animals.

I've had people describe their animals in spirit as their soul animal, soul mate or heart animal. It's interesting because with the language they're using to say this they understand on a subconscious level that they have this soul connection with their animal's soul. Consciously they are not aware of the lifetimes that they have shared together or know how long their souls have been connected. It's just another incredible fact that animals have helped me to understand.

I've also been asked if it's possible for souls of humans that we've had lifetimes with to reincarnate in our animals. This can sound very farfetched and bizarre but I've had numerous experiences now during my conversations with animals where they have disclosed who they really are. I have a number of clients where we have worked out that it is a grandparent or parent or child whose soul aspect is in their animal. This means that the soul that had a human lifetime has now come back in an animal body for another lifetime and stay connected with the human they've known.

I have been asked to have conversations with living animals who are vocally very chatty, and have discovered that sometimes they are trying to tell their humans who they really are!

Ragamuffin's story

Ragamuffin

I had a conversation with a lady whose cat Ragamuffin was exhibiting changed bathroom etiquette and was being very vocal. She didn't know why he was behaving like this or what he was trying to say.

Changing behaviour is one of the most effective methods animals have to let you know that something is wrong or that they want you to know something. When you haven't mastered telepathic communication, they rely on facial expression, body language, vocalisations or changes in behaviour to get your attention, and it's so clever that they know to do this. Changing their toileting behaviour is very noticeable. Interestingly when I talk with animals demonstrating this change they are not being deliberately naughty – they are trying to communicate.

CHAPTER 3: Soul connections

I received an intuitive message that the cat was trying to tell Mum who he was. I felt it was a human she had known. Mum listed a number of names for me but nothing resonated. Then she said a first and second name together and all my hairs stood on end – I was receiving confirmation that this was the soul who was in her cat.

Surprisingly the soul was of her first son who had been born prematurely after a complicated pregnancy and he sadly passed away not long after. The family had addressed him by his first and middle names together. After discovering this amazing connection, Mum explained how Ragamuffin came to join them.

Her family were out for the day and had walked into a pet store. They weren't actually looking for another animal, just browsing. Her second son, who had been born some time after her first son passed away, looked at this cat and announced that the family had to take him home. Her son didn't know why he felt this, and Mum didn't know, but they took the cat with them and Ragamuffin was finally reunited with his Mum.

Ragamuffin absolutely adored his human brother and got distressed when his brother moved away and only came back for brief visits. Part of his behaviour change was related to being upset with the absence of his brother. The other part was trying to tell his Mum who he was. I was surprised when Mum shared that her first son had a complication with his renal system, and here was Ragamuffin expressing his feelings with his renal system. It all made sense.

Once Mum acknowledged who he is, his excessive vocalising settled and his bathroom etiquette returned to normal. His message had been heard and understood and responded to, so he could go back to behaving normally knowing his Mum knows who he is.

CHAPTER 4

Preparing For Goodbye

CHAPTER 4
Preparing For Goodbye

Saying goodbye to our animals is never easy, but when we have some warning that their time to pass is close, we can use the remaining time to make them as happy as possible.

Sadly we never know how long our animals are going to be staying with us. We need to appreciate that every day we get to spend with them is precious and we cannot take their presence for granted.

Your pet may have favourite places they like to visit, such as the beach, nature walks, dog friendly cafes, friends' homes or parks. You can bring your animal so much joy by including these activities.

They may have special humans and other animals that they love to visit and interact with or they may love having their favourite humans and animals come to visit them at home. You can spoil them with their favourite treats.

You can take time just to be with them - they love your undivided attention and spending quality 1:1 time with you. Playing favourite games and playing with their favourite toys can provide joy for you and them – try and video these interactions if you can. If you have other animals, continue your 1:1 time with them as well so that they don't feel left out. They will understand that something is going on but need their routines maintained and continue to need love from you too. Let them know what is happening so that they have time to prepare for farewells.

CHAPTER 4: Preparing for goodbye

My most important suggestion is to take lots of photos and videos of your animal and of you with them. You can't take too many. When they pass away the grief may be too intense and your emotions too raw to be able to look at their images straight away. When the pain starts to ease, having these memories and especially the videos is so helpful. When my cat Paddy passed away it was too upsetting for some time to look at the last photos I had taken with him. When I was ready to look, I found videos that I didn't even remember taking. It was just wonderful seeing and hearing him interacting and eternally alive.

I now have deliberately taken videos of my cats vocalising, purring and playing. They are all still young and healthy but these are irreplaceable experiences and moments together that I want to capture and remember forever.

CHAPTER 5

Dealing with Animal Bereavement and Grief

CHAPTER 5
Dealing with Animal Bereavement and Grief

Having to say goodbye to animals is one of the most difficult things that you do. You feel as though your heart has shattered. How can you possibly heal? How can you move on and resume some normality of life? Animal parents describe having a hole in their heart. There are reminders of your animals everywhere - their food bowls, their toys and even reminders of their hair or fur or feathers which appear in strange places long after they pass.

Grief is such an individual experience. There is no set timeline for when you should recover from an animal's passing. You need to acknowledge the feelings that you feel and do what you need to do to cope with your loss. When you are ready it can be really helpful looking at photographs and videos and seeing your animals when they were healthy and talking to you and playing. Having those memories of happier times can help with the recovery. There are also lots of ways to remember animals with different memorials and items that remind you of them. You can have their paw prints captured in artwork or incorporate some of their fur or ashes into jewellery. There are different ways that you can honour the impact that they've had on your life and always remember them.

There's no denying that the loss of an animal is difficult for you. It's difficult for the other human members of the family, it's difficult for the other animal members of the family, and difficult for the animal who passes over. Everyone is grieving. Your animals who are still with you will know that you need comforting and will try

CHAPTER 5: Dealing with animal bereavement and grief

to do that but they will need comforting too. They will be looking to you to comfort them. Your animals in spirit will know that you are grieving and they wish that they could come and physically comfort you.

It is emotionally challenging working out what you want to do or what you should do when you have an elderly animal or an animal who is extremely unwell. I've had animal parents querying if they made the right choice with euthanasia and many people hold on to guilt and regret about the decisions they made at the end. I've spoken with numerous animals in spirit and none of them hold grudges or regret the decisions that their humans have made on their behalf. They know that you act out of love and that you don't want them being in pain or suffering unnecessarily. It's an unfortunate circumstance that your animals don't live as long as you do so dealing with their passing is something that you go through even though you never want to have to say goodbye. Sometimes the decision is taken out of your hands if animals pass traumatically such as in car accidents or like my cat Reilly having an unexpected heart attack. These situations are particularly difficult because you don't get a chance to say goodbye and thank your animal for being in your life and sharing so much love. You have to deal with the shock as well as the grief.

One of the things animals can do after they have gone through a healing phase on the other side is to pay you an energetic visit. They haven't explained how they do this yet but somehow they can put on a temporary physical body so that you can recognise them. A number of people have seen their animals running up and down their corridors. To me this makes no sense because the physical body no longer exists but it's a reality. For animals in spirit it's a way to reassure you that their soul has transitioned safely and it gives them comfort to come back and visit their family. Your existing animals will definitely know when the animal in spirit comes for a visit. They are much more sensitive to energetic frequencies than we are. In addition to making a visual appearance, your animals in spirit can also vocalise while they are visiting. My cat Reilly would meow when she came for a visit and my boy cats were definitely aware of her presence in the house. I've had other clients reporting that they've heard vocalisations from their animals including birds tweeting.

Animals can also let us know that they are there through physical contact. A number of people have felt their animals jump on their beds or they've felt their animal walking on the bed or felt their animal's body pressure against their body or felt them actually tapping them on the arm or on the face. My cat Paddy plays with my hair when he comes for a visit. He used to lie on my pillow as a kitten and gently massage my hair with his paws. It's reassuring to have this sign that he's with me. I've also had someone tell me that she smells her animal when she visits. She had a very distinctive sweet scent which she recognises. Whether you see them, hear them, feel them, or smell them, your animals have a variety of ways to come back and visit you which is lovely for you and for them.

They can also do things to make noises in the house so that you are aware of their presence or they can move things such as their toys so that you know that something has changed during the night. It's normally early in the morning when your animals visit

CHAPTER 5: Dealing with animal bereavement and grief

you energetically because that's the easiest time for them to be able to transition from the spiritual plane to our earth plane. You might feel as though you were dreaming or hallucinating or that it's wishful thinking feeling that you've connected with your animal or being aware of their presence. I would like to reassure you that these are genuine experiences when your animal returns for a temporary visit. They can be highly creative in letting you know that they are with you.

Tigerlily (p.31 in Chapter 2) when she was alive used to sit behind the window blinds in her Mum's bedroom and wobble them which Mum said makes a terribly loud noise. She has continued to do this on her energetic visits to let Mum know without a doubt that she is there. When it happens for the first time it can give you quite a fright because you can't see anything but you can definitely hear it.

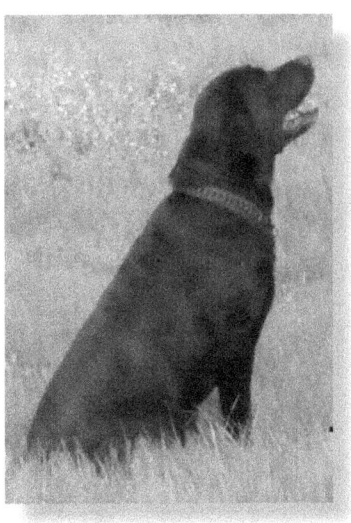

Tyson

A friend posted on social media that her dog Tyson had passed away. I looked at his photo and he said, "Tell Mum I'm coming for a visit tonight." Now this was the night on the day he passed. Usually animals go through healing for some time before they can return for an energetic visit, but he was absolutely certain that he was coming back that night. I duly passed on the message to his Mum who wasn't surprised, and she told me that he was a very evolved soul. I sent her a message a few days later to find out what had happened. She laughed and said that he had jumped on the bed with such force that he knocked two pillows off! Because he had only passed that day she had temporarily forgotten that and had automatically put out her hand to pat him, then remembered that he wasn't there. It was so wonderful that he could come back so quickly and confirm that his soul was safe.

Thor

CHAPTER 5: Dealing with animal bereavement and grief

Mum had been struggling with the sudden loss of her gorgeous young male cat Thor. She really wanted him to come back and reassure her that he was okay. I encouraged her to keep talking out loud to him and inviting him to visit.

A few days after he passed I received this message from her:

"Oh my goodness I don't know what to say.

Last night I heard Thor's trill (unique vocalisation of Maine Coon cats) but I didn't say anything. I thought it was in my mind.

This morning I woke up to a cat jumping on my bed...but no one was there.

Then brushing my teeth I felt a cat brush past my leg. I looked down expecting to see a cat. No one was there.

Then this afternoon I was working at my table and felt a paw on my knee. I reached out to pat a cat expecting it to be Thor's brother. There was no one there.

When I told my husband this afternoon and begged him not to think I'm crazy he said that he heard Thor trill last night too and he believed what I felt!"

Given that Thor was so young, I was impressed that he was able to come back for an energetic visit so quickly after his passing, and this provided so much comfort for his humans.

Charley

One of the most startling energetic visits was from Charley, a dog in spirit who had enjoyed a lifetime of mutual teasing with her Mum. Mum was cleaning one day and suddenly heard the doggy door crashing, and knew there were no dogs there. She said she nearly had a heart attack as there was nothing to see. The hairs on her arms stood up which is her recognition sign when Charley is visiting energetically so she worked out what was happening. Charley was being the ultimate tease! Our animals in spirit can still let their personalities come through in conversations and visits.

In addition to energetic visits, animals in spirit can also connect with you through meditations and dreams. I've personally experienced this many times and for me it's just fabulous being able to pick up my cats and genuinely feel them in my arms. I can feel their bodies moving with their breathing and can hear them vocalising. You can look into their eyes and connect with them. It is such an amazing accomplishment that they can come to you like that, confirming that their soul is safe, that their souls live on and

CHAPTER 5: Dealing with animal bereavement and grief

that the love bond that you have with them endures. It does help your grieving process to know that their souls endure, that you can always connect with them, and that there is no true separation when they pass away. Yes, they are in the spiritual plane and you exist in the physical plane but they can traverse the planes and connect with you.

You can't command animals to come and visit you but you can certainly invite them to visit. Animals in spirit do hear you when you talk out loud to them so I would encourage you to invite them to visit you. This could be an energetic visit or an appearance in dreams or meditations. They will hear you inviting them and they will come through when they can. Many animal parents are very eager to reconnect with their animals in spirit as soon as possible but sometimes you have to be patient while they heal. Having these experiences with your animals in spirit certainly helps with grief because you get to connect with them instead of fearing that you have lost them forever.

Having a conversation with your animals just before they pass away or when they have passed away means you can ask about their preferences for end-of-life arrangements. Do they want to be cremated? Do they want to be buried? Do they want to have particular trees or plants near them in the garden? Do they want a particular funeral urn? Do they want to have their ashes scattered somewhere significant? Is there anything specific that they would like in their funeral urn? Do they have other suggestions for memorials?

My cats requested specific urns so I played detective to find exactly what they wanted. Paddy and Reilly both requested particular crystals to go with their ashes in the urns and they requested where they wanted their urns located. I've recently connected with a dog who provided very explicit information about the funeral urn that she wanted and she requested to have her favourite squeaky toy in the urn with her ashes. Another dog requested to be buried with lots of flowers so Mum arranged a burial site and she and her friends have planted lots of different flower plants near the grave. It gives animal parents peace knowing that they can honour their animals' requests.

Emily's story

Emily

I first met Emily in 2022 when she had a number of health issues and Mum wanted to understand what was happening. Emily and

CHAPTER 5: Dealing with animal bereavement and grief

I had a fascinating conversation where she revealed that she was taking on family karmic issues and health issues for her human Mum, and her Mum's Mum. The only issue that was genuinely hers was anxiety, and she was only anxious because she was worrying about her Mum! As a small dog, Emily was struggling with the quantity of health issues she was taking on and admitted she had taken on too much. She also let me understand that she is an empath and is very sensitive to human health issues.

Fortunately Emily and her Mum were able to sort things out so that Emily and her Mum both got healthier and developed a much deeper connection. Emily told me that she was here to support her Mum's spiritual development and loved watching her progress.

Mum recently contacted me as Emily's health had deteriorated and she intuitively felt that Emily would be passing over soon. She had questions about end-of-life arrangements and Emily's preferences for how to spend her remaining time. Emily confirmed that she would be passing within the next 2 months. She wanted to be cremated and gave instructions for her urn and special crystals. She wanted walks somewhere quiet in nature and dog chocolate! She already knew that she was going to reincarnate as a different dog breed.

I was contacted by Mum again just before Emily passed to convey more messages and pass on Emily's spiritual guidance for Mum. Emily passed away earlier than expected as the body she was coming back in was available earlier than anticipated. Mum had purchased her urn as requested and has set up a beautiful shrine for Emily. Emily had provided a date by which time she expected Mum would find her in her new body. Although Mum searched diligently, she was unable to find the rescue dog that Emily had described near to the deadline. When I checked with Emily to see what was happening, she'd had to find a different body to swap into as the first one was not available.

I've experienced this personally and with clients – sometimes things happen beyond the animal's control and plans don't proceed. Although this is a setback when you have been waiting patiently (or impatiently!) for their return, animals do everything they can to reunite with you. Emily had found a puppy body to swap into and was still within the timeframe she had set. Mum asked what she'd prefer as her new name. She chose 'Lila', as she loves the Sanskrit meaning "Divine play" alluding to her soul connection with her Mum and her role with Mum's soul growth. Mum also asked Emily for a sign that she was close.

Although the puppy was available when Mum contacted the owner, again things changed and the adoption was unable to proceed. Having the anticipation build up twice and then be disappointed was such an anticlimax and emotionally tough to deal with. Mum decided to take matters into her own hands and searched for available dogs near her. She found a puppy that looked very similar to what Emily had shown me in our earlier conversation. In the photo Mum sent me the puppy had a lilac collar. The female puppy and her sister were both available. Mum asked me to ask Emily if her soul could swap into the puppy with the lilac collar, and wanted to find out if she'd like her sister to come with her. Emily needed some time to negotiate with the soul in the lilac collared puppy. The soul in situ has to agree to swap out and return to Heaven allowing the other soul to swap in to return to their human family. Fortunately the soul in the lilac collared

CHAPTER 5: Dealing with animal bereavement and grief

puppy agreed, on the proviso that her sister would be adopted with Emily's soul in the new puppy so that they could stay together. Mum was absolutely thrilled and arranged the adoption of both dogs straight away.

Lila

There was so much synchronicity with this outcome. Mum had requested a sign from Emily. Emily's first collar was lilac, and the puppy's collar is lilac. The name Lila that Emily chose for her new incarnation also means lilac. Emily had already asked her new sister what she'd like to be called, and she chose 'Tahlia.'

Mum now has Lila and Tahlia at home. She said she felt overwhelmed but was really happy holding Lila for the first time. Lila settled in at home straight away and started playing with her old toys. Mum sent me a selfie of her with Lila – I'm not sure who looks more contented. As I said to Mum, it's the end of the chapter with Emily, and the start of a whole new story with Lila and Tahlia.

Ben's story

Ben

Ben is one of the few clients I got to meet in person. I usually connect with animals through photographs, so it was a novelty and pleasure to meet and spend time with him. Ben is a very gentle old soul who absolutely adored his Mum. He had some significant obstacles in his life with health issues, but continued living life as fully as he could supporting Mum and pouring out his love to her.

He had a hilarious sense of humour - he described himself as a trussed up turkey after being bound with bandages after a procedure. The image of him being a turkey provided some much needed mirth given his health status and prognosis.

He was determined to stay as long as he possibly could to be with his human Mum and support her life purpose. Both of them knew that his time was near, but he said that every day he stayed was a gift for him to spend it with his Mum.

Saying goodbye to your animals is one of the most difficult and heartbreaking things you do. Your animals have loved you unconditionally, supported you through your challenges, snuggled with you, made you laugh, protected you and have been your non-judgmental and loyal companions.

I asked Mum to take videos of Ben as that helped me with my grief journey when I was ready to reminisce. I also suggested that she take some selfies with him and she now has some lovely images of the two of them together.

Ben told me when it was his time to go to the other side. His Mum had the opportunity to spend time thanking him for being with her as long as he had been, for supporting her in so many ways, and for his love.

Ben had time to advise of his wishes for afterwards. He asked that a piece of green turquoise be placed with his ashes. Green turquoise has many metaphysical properties including healing, and can support calmness and courage, traits which he exhibited.

After he passed at home peacefully outside under the trees, he shared an image of him walking freely, and wagging his tail, full of energy. His soul still had a process of healing to go through, but he wanted to reassure his Mum that he had transitioned safely and was okay.

Our animals are incredibly grateful for the opportunity to share our lives, and for the love and security they experience being part of our family. I felt privileged to have the opportunity of supporting Mum and her beloved dog Ben as he gained his angel wings and commenced his new life on the other side. He has told us that he is coming back as a dog.

Coco's story

Coco

CHAPTER 5: Dealing with animal bereavement and grief

Coco is a very gentle soul who avoided conflict and in her later years loved spending time sunbaking in the garden and spending time lying near crystals.

She had a number of complex health issues and Mum wanted to find out what was happening and what she wanted done. She described a number of conditions and requested that Mum continue the Reiki and other healing modalities that she was using as they were helping her to feel more comfortable. She didn't want any active medical treatment as she knew her time to pass was close. She wanted to stay at home and pass over on her terms when she was ready. She was sad to be leaving her Mum because she loved being with her. Coco requested to be cremated, and wanted to have lemurian crystals near her ashes.

She spent hours in the garden every day with her fur brother and spent a lot of time under a wormwood plant.

Mum could tell her time was getting closer and her breathing changed. Mum spent hours lying with her in the garden and in bed not knowing which day would be her last. Every time Mum put her hand on Coco to check her, she would start purring. She transitioned peacefully after the June Solstice this year. Mum has a piece of wormwood and lemurian crystals near her ashes as she requested. Reassuringly Mum has felt Coco lying on her bed numerous times since she left.

Delilah's story

Delilah

I had a conversation with Delilah in late 2022. She was experiencing some health issues and Mum knew that her time was approaching, and wanted answers to her questions. She revealed that she had had former lifetimes with her Mum. I was trying to find out her name in one of the lifetimes but she was playing games with me and said, "B." Often animals create puzzles for me with their answers, and I have to work out the solution. She wouldn't give me any more letters or say her name, then joked that it was 'Brunhilda'! Mum worked out who she was.

CHAPTER 5: Dealing with animal bereavement and grief

She was anticipating that she would pass three months after our conversation. She knew her health was declining and she felt tired. She said her Mum would know when it was her time to leave. Delilah was able to confirm her end-of-life wishes – she wanted to be cremated and have her ashes in an urn. Before then, she wanted to spend time in a garden smelling the plants.

Her special message to Mum was "Don't be too sad when I go – it's been a full life, I have no regrets and have my heart full of love from you and for you." She wanted Mum to know how happy she was to have had another lifetime with her.

She managed to stay for months longer than she told us. In her last few days she got to do some special activities. She went swimming in a lake and got to have her own bowl of ice cream with a cone! She got to sniff the plants.

It makes saying goodbye a little bit easier knowing you are respecting their wishes and fulfilling their requests for some special moments that are so memorable for you.

Arranging a conversation with your animal in spirit (mediumship) can significantly help with the grief process. You may feel overwhelmed with grief, guilt, regret or remorse and don't know how you can possibly move forward. You may feel as though your heart can never recover. You may crave connection with your animal in spirit and receive confirmation that their soul has transitioned safely. You may want to delve deeper into your relationship with your animal and understand why you had such a strong soul connection and discover your purpose for being together.

There are so many questions that bereaved animal parents want answered:

- Are you okay? What happened?
- Have you forgiven me? Was it the right time?
- Do you know how much I love you?
- Do you know how much I want to hug you one more time?
- What's it like where you are?
- Did you send me a new animal to help me heal?
- Is it too soon to get another animal?
- Have you been with me before in this lifetime?
- Have you had past lifetimes with me in human or animal form?
- Why were you here? What was your mission?
- What were your soul lessons?
- Were you here to help me with my soul lessons?
- Are you going to reincarnate?
- Can you hear me when I talk out loud to you?
- What messages or guidance do you have for me?

The messages from your animals are heartwarming and comforting. They want you to know that they hold no regrets, apart from having to leave you, or if they passed without the opportunity to say goodbye. They know how much you love them and how much you miss them. They send messages about how deeply they love you. They express gratitude for your love and care. They thank

CHAPTER 5: Dealing with animal bereavement and grief

you for the toys and games and fun. They are so grateful that you were their humans. They appreciate being a valued member of the family. They want you to understand that there is nothing to forgive. They don't want you holding onto remorse and guilt for the decisions made at the end. They don't mean to cause distress when they have to leave.

They express sorrow knowing that you grieve. They are grieving too. Sometimes their bodies and illness prevented them from staying for longer. Some of them hide the extent of their illness and pain for as long as possible because they don't want you worrying, and they want to defer saying goodbye for as long as they possibly can. My cat Paddy hid organ failure for some time. He kept doing all of his normal activities right up till the day before he was ready to pass over.

They can also confirm if they have been visiting energetically if you are not quite convinced that it really was them that you thought you saw, heard or felt. Most excitingly they can advise that they are coming back when they know that they are definitely reincarnating. They can then provide the necessary information so that their humans can find them in their new body and bring them home.

There are so many benefits of having a mediumship conversation. The ultimate outcome is being at peace with the passing of your animal. Having the clarity and relief from having your questions answered means that you can experience a more positive and calmer mindset. You can have a brighter roadmap for the future, without staying stuck in deep, prolonged grief. Your heart can heal with receiving personal messages from your animal which is healing for them too.

You can receive advice from your animal about your own spiritual development and growth, and they can continue to teach and guide you from the other side. You can gain a deeper understanding of the soul connections with your animal in this lifetime and in the past, and ask them about future connections.

Through mediumship you have the opportunity for ongoing communication with your animals in spirit. Animals have taught that the soul endures and is always contactable. They help us to understand that the love relationship you have with them also endures. There is no true separation when they pass over – you have an eternal conduit of connection with them.

Other options to help with animal bereavement include joining in person or online pet loss support groups. There are also grief counsellors specially trained to help people to cope with animal loss.

As a clinical aromatherapist I am aware that therapeutic grade essential oils such as Frankincense and Rose can support emotional wellbeing at this difficult time. As a crystal therapist I love using lepidolite and danburite crystals to support animals and humans through the emotional upheaval we undergo when an animal passes away.

It's so important to consider the impact of bereavement on your living animals. They too will be grieving and missing their fellow animal. This loss can have a profound and long-lasting effect on them.

CHAPTER 5: Dealing with animal bereavement and grief

Willow's story

Willow

I was asked to have a conversation with a lovely dog called Willow who had lost her older dog sister two months previously. Her Mum wanted to know how she was coping without her sister, as the unexpected passing had significantly affected the whole family, human and animal.

Willow told me, "She's left a huge hole in our family. In a way I feel lost without my big sister. She was a wonderful role model and I miss her wisdom as well as her presence." She told me that her sister left big footsteps to fill, and I love the synchronicity of all the paw prints surrounding her in the photo that her Mum sent me. She shared that taking on the alpha female role in her sister's absence feels like a big responsibility and she sometimes doubts herself. Her sister trusted her and believed in her and this is inspiring her to take on the leadership mantle. Willow is committed to undertaking this role with the best intentions to honour her sister's legacy.

The intensity of grief she was dealing with brought tears to my eyes – she let me feel what she is feeling. Having her sister visit energetically helps, but she wishes her sister could stay. Mum told me that Willow will only go to sleep at night now if she is touching her – she seeks the reassurance of the connection and this behaviour has intensified with the passing of her sister. Mum often talks to Willow about her sister so that they are remembering her and acknowledging her contribution to the family.

Saying goodbye to her sister has had a huge impact on Willow's life. She is aware that the rest of the family is coping with grief too, and wants to be able to support them. She was very grateful that her Mum wanted to check how she was managing in the aftermath of her loss.

It takes time to work through grief and to adjust to not having that loved soul physically with you.

Key wisdom:

- Animals can grieve for a considerable time, just as humans do.

- Unless the animals tell us, we can't comprehend how the experience of loss affects them, how intensely they feel the separation or the length of time they endure and process these strong emotions. Unresolved or protracted grief may result in physical symptoms or behaviour changes. Fortunately there

CHAPTER 5: Dealing with animal bereavement and grief

are healing modalities available now to assist animals with emotional issues so that they can have their burdens lifted.

Remi's story

Remi

I was asked to connect with Remi as her human parents were concerned about some odd behaviour. Remi let me feel what was happening on a physical level so that I could tell her parents what was going on with her musculoskeletal system, and potential management options to assist her.

Unexpectedly during the conversation Remi revealed that she was grieving for a soul in spirit. She said that she had a twin who died in utero and this really affected her. I understand that twin pregnancies in horses are rare and that survival of both twins is even rarer. Remi let me feel the intensity of her grief she was still dealing with years after her twin passed away. She admitted that the unresolved grief along with other factors was contributing to depression. She recognised that she was exhausted emotionally and physically, and needed vitality.

I was able to pass on this key information to Remi's parents so that they could arrange appropriate support for her physical and emotional issues, allowing her to release these burdens and enjoy life again. It's hard to tell from external appearances what our animals are dealing with emotionally and psychologically. It is so beneficial when they are brave enough to disclose really personal details with a stranger so that they can get help and not remain stuck in emotional turmoil.

CHAPTER 6

Animals' Perspectives On Reincarnation

CHAPTER 6
Animals' Perspectives On Reincarnation

I was intrigued to find out what animals feel about the experience of reincarnating, having had at least one lifetime on Earth, and then passing over. I consulted my cats who have reincarnated, and other reincarnated animal clients for their unique views about their experiences.

Our animals are yearning to come back to us. They explain that having a new body is like wearing a new suit. They have to adjust to how to move in it and explore their flexibility. A cat who was fairly immobile before he passed came back in a very energetic, strong kitten body and has jumped and leapt to great heights because he can and he is revelling in his new athleticism and freedom to explore. The cat who came back as a dog had to realise and adjust to the fact that as a dog he can't leap up onto his humans' bed like he used to, so now uses his set of stairs to reach his destination independently.

One of my cats described the interesting experience swapping into a kitten body several months after birth and swapping gender. She appreciated my diligence with searching for her so that she could come home to me.

When they return in their new bodies, animals have a different scent. Animals are very scent aware so initially may not be receptive or accept the new arrival because they don't recognise their smell. The other animal family members have to recognise them on a soul level as physically they may look very different to

CHAPTER 6: Animals' perspectives on reincarnation

their previous incarnation, their familiar scent has gone, and they may be a different gender and telepathically communicate with a completely different and foreign voice.

The animals who have reincarnated recognise and know their human family members and animal family members. When they return they know the layout of the house – they know where to sleep, where to eat, where the bathroom is and where their toys are. They are also familiar with your common phrases such as "Are you ready for breakfast?"

Animals are craving the physical reunion with their humans just as much as the humans are. Animals describe this as "the highlight." They have watched their humans grieve. They can then witness the incredulous looks and the overwhelming love and relief when their humans hold them in their arms again and really know it's their animal's soul and not just a dream or wishful thinking. One of my cats remarked, "It is radical that we can come back and many humans have not comprehended or experienced this reality."

CHAPTER 7

Welcoming Your Animal Home

CHAPTER 7
Welcoming Your Animal Home

Knowing that animal souls can reincarnate has changed so many lives and helped so many parents move through their grief process. There are no words to describe the depth of emotions seeing and holding your reincarnated animal for the first time.

Lucky Jr's story

Lucky Jr

The power of love

I met Dad at what could really be described as a very low point in his life. His beautiful female dog Keumjoo, who he described as his "princess and four-legged daughter" had passed away five

CHAPTER 7: Welcoming your animal home

months earlier. Dad said his "world fell apart that day that we said goodbye to her."

Their equally precious male dog Lucky Jr had known Keumjoo since he was a baby and losing her took a toll on him as well. The family decided to rescue a little girl dog from South Korea. Lucky Jr and Tannie didn't develop the same close bond that he and Keumjoo had shared, but at least he had a companion.

The family experienced another tragic blow five months after Keumjoo's passing. Dad told me that "out of nowhere and without warning my precious baby boy dog Lucky Jr died suddenly and unexpectedly. He was only 5 years old and he was my beloved four-legged boy, my buddy, my alarm clock and my work mate. We were shattered and devastated." Dad admitted that he was depressed, distraught with deep grief and couldn't understand why both of his dogs had left in quick succession. He had questions and he needed answers.

I had a conversation with Lucky Jr in spirit. He was happy to chat and answer Dad's questions, including the circumstances surrounding his passing.

Excitingly he told me that he was going to reincarnate and come home to his family before Christmas so that he would be there to celebrate with them. He said he would be a rescue dog and would be changing gender to come back as a female Samoyed. Since Dad and his daughter had searched local rescue agencies without success, I suggested that they search for Samoyed rescue organizations.

Poppy

Dad sent me a photo of a rescue female Samoyed they had found at the Samoyed Rescue Southern California. He wanted me to confirm if this was the dog that Lucky Jr's soul would reincarnate into. Lucky Jr told me that his soul would swap into her when the adoption proceeded. The family christened her 'Poppy.' She looks very similar to Lucky Jr. Dad said, "Some people may not have an open mind about this, but I do not rule anything out."

Although Dad contacted the SRSC several times to discuss adoption, there were hurdles to overcome being out of state, and Dad feared that he would not reunite with his baby boy. He was advised that "they couldn't allow the adoption to proceed without a meet and greet."

After numerous discussions with SRSC and his family, Dad made his decision. He said, "I knew that the only way I was going to be able to adopt Poppy and have my precious baby boy back was to

CHAPTER 7: Welcoming your animal home

go there and meet these folks and my new four-legged daughter." Dad flew from Iowa to Southern California, rented a car and went to meet Poppy.

"As soon as I arrived and walked around the corner Poppy ran to me and hugged me and started kissing me. She knew me and I knew instantly that my boy had come back. I had taken a couple of his favourite toys with me on the plane as I wanted to see her reaction to them, and she immediately played with them."

The rescue staff had not witnessed a reaction like this. Dad commented, "I signed the adoption legal papers and with joyous goodbyes from everyone at K9 City and the gracious ladies from SRSC I left with our new family member and started driving back 1900 miles to Iowa with my girl Poppy." He said he and Poppy had time to reconnect and bond during the drive. He said that she would just lean her body against his. It must be wonderful to feel and smell your human after a separation.

Interestingly Poppy is not a Samoyed. Lucky Jr was smart enough to tell his family that he was so that they would find him in his new female body. It defies logic but the information helped his humans to locate him, adopt him and bring him home.

Poppy settled back home within two days. Watching them playing, Dad said, "Poppy and her dog sister Tannie act as if they have been sisters since babies." It has been a delight listening to Dad laughing at their antics in the videos he has taken of them playing together in the snow.

This heartfelt message from him sums up the whole experience: "I'm so grateful that Lucky Jr told us he was coming back, and that finally he was able to return to us. Poppy is part of our family until the end of time."

Key wisdom:

- Having an animal mediumship conversation can really assist the grief process for humans and animals. The animal parents can gain peace of mind about the reasons for passing. Animals have good medical knowledge and can describe what happened. They don't want us holding on to guilt, remorse, or regret that we should have picked up health issues sooner and perhaps we could have started treatment earlier and extended their life.

- Celebrating Christmas and other family events without our animals can be challenging. We really miss their presence, their vocalisations and participation. Know that they will be watching from the other side and be open to sensing that they are with you. Having their photos at the events can help you feel that they are being included. Lucky Jr knew what a difference it would make being able to join his family for Christmas, which he did.

- Rescue animals seem to intuitively know to try and come back as a rescue animal as they know that's who their humans are more likely to adopt. I have been asked if their soul swaps into a body that has been traumatized if they are affected by what happened in the past. My understanding is that it is the soul who was in the rescue animal body when the trauma happened who experienced that. When an animal soul reincarnates, their soul moves into the physical body and any memories of the past belong to the soul who has vacated. Emotions from trauma may remain in cellular memory impacting the incoming soul, but these can be released.

CHAPTER 7: Welcoming your animal home

- Just as in Poppy's journey, some animals defer swapping their souls into their new body until they are sure that they will be reunited with their family. If something doesn't work out with the adoption they can negotiate to swap into another body and it saves disturbing the current soul inhabiting the body until everything is confirmed.

Winston's story

Winston

Mum's St Bernard boy Winston passed away almost 6 years ago. He was very loved and Mum was keen to connect with him.

When I had a conversation with Winston he shared that he and his Mum had been together in previous lifetimes, and he has had human and animal incarnations with her. He was aware that Mum was still grieving for him and asked that she "keep loving me and I will keep loving her."

Encouragingly he said, "We will have future lives together. She's a beautiful soul, and we will keep reconnecting." He didn't indicate when those future lives would be or if he was going to reincarnate again in this lifetime with his Mum.

Some time later, another of Mum's dogs, JayCee, exhibited some unusual behaviour staring at Mum and pressing his chin on her hand. Mum is very intuitive and knew he was trying to tell her something important. When I spoke with JayCee, he explained that he was being a messenger for Winston. Winston was ready to reincarnate and wanted his Mum to know that he was coming back as a female Weimaraner rescue dog, and for Mum to start searching for him. This was an unexpected conversation for Mum but it was wonderful knowing that her boy was coming back.

Mum started searching for an available female rescue dog as Winston had described, and sent me a photo of the prospective new family member. Unfortunately the adoption did not proceed as the surrendering family found a new home for their dog only blocks away from where they lived. Although this meant that the dog could continue her relationship with her original family, it was disappointing for Mum to think she had found Winston, and then lost the opportunity to reconnect. Winston had to start looking for a different option to return to his family.

During our animal communication mentorship sessions recently, Winston connected with his Mum and told her that he was coming back as a rescue St Bernard male puppy, about 3 months old, and that she would find him within the next month. This was such exciting news, and again Mum started her search to find Winston in his new body. She found the most adorable rescue puppy of the right age in the right time frame and sent me a photo. I received confirmation that this was the body that Winston would reincarnate in, but his soul hadn't swapped in as he was waiting for Mum to find him. I was thrilled for Mum and the puppy!

CHAPTER 7: Welcoming your animal home

Charlie

Dad flew halfway across the USA to meet the puppy, who provided several names to choose from and has been christened 'Charlie.' Charlie and Dad had to stay overnight at a motel before starting the long drive home. Mum was excited to see that he sleeps in the same posture as Winston, with his front paw tucked under him.

Charlie settled back home very quickly, even choosing to sleep on the same couch where Winston used to sleep. Although all of the other dogs joined the family after Winston's passing, Charlie has bonded with them and particularly loves playing with older brother Tuukka. Mum sees more and more of Winston's characteristics becoming evident as he grows. He continues to lie with his front paw tucked under and the same back leg extended behind him as Winston did. He also has started doing 'the lean' against his humans' legs as Winston did. He makes the same slurping noises when he drinks and walks away from the water bowl leaving a trail of water behind him. All of these behaviours are evoking memories of Winston.

As she was curious about Charlie's breed and heritage, Mum arranged a DNA test for him. Charlie has several different breeds in his genetics, but surprisingly the results showed he has 0% St Bernard genes ! I am so impressed with Winston's wisdom telling Mum that he would be a St Bernard rescue puppy, because he knew she would find him even though he wasn't that breed.

Winston was adopted after the puppy stage so Mum is loving watching Charlie grow and play, although a little less enthusiastic about the current "chew everything" phase. After the loss and grief she experienced, Mum is just so happy and grateful that Charlie is with her, and they can share another lifetime together.

Key learnings:

- There is no guideline of time for our animals to reincarnate. They have shown me that when they pass over to the other side they go through a significant healing process. Once this is completed they can return for energetic visits to spend time with their families. Some animals have the opportunity to reincarnate very quickly after their passing and for others there is a delay. With Winston there was a significant gap till he found the Weimaraner body, and when that didn't eventuate, there was another delay till he found Charlie's body to swap into. Animals have taught me that when it is their destiny to return, they will keep trying until they succeed. They are as eager for the reunion as we are.

- The delays and having to potentially swap in and out of a few bodies mean our animals are negotiating with existing souls in bodies so that they can swap in and be with their families.

CHAPTER 7: Welcoming your animal home

In some cases where the first attempt has not worked, the animal's soul has waited till their humans have found them before swapping into the next body to ensure that they are swapping into the physical body that they are definitely going to reincarnate in. When the planned reincarnation doesn't proceed, it's a tough time for the humans who have been waiting in anticipation for their loved animal to return. Our animals do everything they can to find a suitable body as quickly as they can. They and their families have to be patient so that they can reunite in the physical realm.

- There is so much excitement to be experienced when the reincarnated animal displays the idiosyncrasies and quirky behaviours of our former animals. They do what they can to confirm who they really are, and show us how grateful they are to be back with us again.

Maggie & Meep's story

Maggie

I was contacted by a bereaved Mum who'd had two black and white sister cats, Maggie and Daisy. Maggie, affectionately nicknamed Meep, had recently passed away, and Mum wasn't sure if Daisy wanted to be an only cat or if she wanted a companion.

In the inexplicable way that the universe works, Mum had been told about a cat available for adoption who looked very like Maggie except for the location of a black facial marking. Her name was Meep! These weird occurrences happen to me all the time and I'm now used to experiencing phenomena that you just can't rationally explain.

Mum went to meet Meep and was amazed by the reaction when they were introduced. Meep let her hold her, touched her face with her paw and gazed into her eyes with Maggie's eyes. It was soul recognition on a heart level. Meep hadn't responded like that with anyone else.

Meep

CHAPTER 7: Welcoming your animal home

Mum wanted to know if Daisy would be happy to welcome Meep into the family, and wanted to know if Maggie's soul was definitely in Meep to come back to her family. Having Maggie's nickname as her name and her reaction to Mum were very compelling indications that Meep was Maggie.

I had conversations with Daisy and Maggie and asked Mum's questions. Daisy confirmed that she knew Maggie was coming back and wanted her sister home again. Maggie confirmed that her soul was returning to her family in Meep, that she had been having conversations with Daisy, that she was very excited that her Mum had found her, and that she was looking forward to the family reunion. She said, "One lifetime of love isn't enough."

After the conversations Mum told me, "I'm really happy. I'm content with everything and at peace. I'm so grateful for everything right now. My heart is overflowing."

Meep arrived home and settled in very quickly with her Mum and sister. Daisy was keen to meet her and they are now sharing their Mum's bed. Mum updated me after their first week and said, "I can happily say that a week into our adoption all is well, we are loving our new life together." She has since shared that Meep is showing more of Maggie's mannerisms as she adjusts to being home again. Meep and Daisy are sharing space happily, eating side by side and enjoying being together again.

To me it's so fascinating when animal souls reincarnate. They walk back into the house knowing who everyone is (animal and human) and where everything is. Usually within a couple of days they've integrated back into the family, have been accepted by their animal siblings and life returns to normal.

Key wisdom:

- This is an example of when a soul in spirit returns in an older animal. Animals have taught me that the higher evolved aspect of their soul returning to Earth can swap into an animal body at any age. They do not necessarily move into a body when it is conceived. Meep was several years old when Maggie negotiated to swap into her. The existing soul obligingly moves out and returns to the other side.

- Many animal parents like Meep's Mum comment that more of the original animal's traits and behaviours become evident over time. The soul has to adjust to being in a new and unfamiliar body. They may have had illnesses or physical limitations in their last lifetime so it feels so unusual having a body with no restrictions. They are excited to explore the world with their new vitality, flexibility and strength. Over time they feel more comfortable and can then exhibit their former characteristics and unique personality.

- As humans, we adjust quickly to having a new animal in our homes and hearts, but it is a significant experience for our animals whose souls are destined to return to us.

CHAPTER 7: Welcoming your animal home

Milo's story

Milo

The joker's journey

One of my clients said goodbye to her gorgeous boy cat Milo in July last year. He was full of life and mischief and a real character.

Mum wasn't planning to get another cat straight away. Her two female cats were keeping her company but they have very different personalities to their furry angel brother.

In the mysterious way that the Universe operates, Mum was contacted by a friend to see if she would like to adopt a female cat who had been abandoned when her family moved. The cat was called Milo! Mum wasn't sure if it was her Milo who had come back to be with her or if he was arranging this connection from the other side to assist with her grief process and help her heart to heal.

After meeting Milo 2, Mum opened her heart and home to her. She rechristened her 'Mila' to avoid confusion. Mila settled in quickly with her fur sisters and started exhibiting some of Milo's behaviours.

Mila

I had a conversation with Milo in spirit to find out if his soul was back in Mila or if he'd helped Mila to find his Mum. He said, "We are one and the same," confirming that an aspect of his soul had reincarnated. He said he didn't mind what he was called. He was just happy to be back.

Everything was progressing smoothly till Mila had to have some dental work done. Imagine Mum's shock when the vet informed her that Mila is a HE! Milo hadn't disclosed that important fact!

I had to speak with Milo again as Mum had to change Mila's details for registration to male gender, and wanted to know what he wanted to be called since she could no longer call him Mila.

CHAPTER 7: Welcoming your animal home

He was laughing like anything when I started the conversation with him, and he said, "Of course I came back as a boy."

I told him that his Mum wanted to pick a new name for him, and asked if he would he be happy with 'Ollie.' He was highly amused and said, "I'd love to pull her chains and give her some really obnoxious names," but decided not to. He didn't want to be called Oliver because of the Oliver Twist story that he was familiar with.

Our animals are so intelligent and know so much more than we give them credit for. I love it when their senses of humour shine through, although this scenario was completely unexpected!

Milo was happy to be named Ollie and has now been correctly registered as a male.

I suspect he will be laughing for some time about keeping his big secret a secret for so long!

As Ollie he has continued to show more of Milo's cheeky behaviour and naughtiness, including trying to shred Mum's lounge! Despite this, Mum is very grateful to have him home and he's happy to be home.

Key wisdom:

- If animals on the other side are not destined to reincarnate back with their humans, they can help another animal to join the family to assist with healing and overcoming grief. Since animals and humans grieve the loss of an animal, it's such a compassionate act to help the family cope by introducing another animal to love.

- Many animal parents are concerned about the timing of getting another animal. How soon is too soon? Your animals in spirit understand that you are not replacing them or being disrespectful of their life if and when you welcome a new animal home. Your animals in spirit understand the powerful healing that can occur when you open your shattered hearts to love again.

- Things happen for a reason, although they may seem like coincidences. For Mum to lose her boy Milo and then be asked to adopt another cat called Milo there was definitely something more at play. Life works in mysterious ways. I've learnt now to be open and accept all sorts of weird occurrences that you just can't explain logically. We only see the tip of the iceberg of reality, magic and miracles in our world.

- Animals have different voices and personalities just as humans do. It's truly delightful hearing animals laughing as Ollie did and letting us experience their sense of humour.

CHAPTER 8

Eternal Soul Existence

CHAPTER 8
Eternal Soul Existence

For those of you currently experiencing grief with the loss of an animal, please be reassured that the soul of your animal endures and the love relationship that you shared together also endures. When your animals pass over, although their physical body no longer exists, their soul endures forever. This is really comforting for animal parents because it means you can always connect with their soul in spirit regardless of how long ago they passed away. Although they now exist in the spiritual plane and humans exist on the earth or the physical plane, through telepathic communication you can connect with their soul and have a conversation. I've spoken with a dog who passed over more than 20 years ago. There is no time limit on connecting with your animal souls in spirit. Even if an aspect of their soul does reincarnate in a new physical body you can still connect with the aspect of their soul in heaven.

I know I've had soul connections with my cat Paddy for thousands of years and I haven't explored how far back our soul connection goes. I won't be the only one who has had such a long soul connection with an animal. It appears some of us have a soul contract with these special animal souls and that we keep reincarnating together through multiple lifetimes to support each other with our soul purpose and our soul evolvement.

CHAPTER 9

Soul Secrets

CHAPTER 9
Soul Secrets

In addition to the wonder of soul reincarnation, there are other soul facts that animals have explained to me and helped me to experience.

In communicating with animals in spirit who have reincarnated, I now know that I can connect with the aspect of the soul in spirit and connect with the aspect of the soul which has reincarnated. They are parts of the same soul but I hear different voices when I talk with them.

In one of my conversations a cat told me that it was worth the wait to find an almost identical body to come back in. He said, "Part of my soul aspect is existing in the spiritual realm and part of me is in the physical plane and my destiny is to keep teaching and sharing wisdom." They know they have reincarnated. I am in awe of animals' knowledge of spirituality.

To further complicate matters, some animals can have aspects of two souls in them and they have to negotiate who leads different roles and how they make decisions. I understand that wild animal souls can reincarnate in domestic animals. There is still so much to learn about souls and reincarnation. Animals can teach you beyond your current level of comprehension.

CHAPTER 9: Soul secrets

Shadow's story

Shadow

I met Mum after her beautiful cat Shadow had passed away. Shadow was part of the family and a beloved child for Mum and her partner. Shadow lived with them for 6 years, then gained her angel wings suddenly. Her passing deeply affected them, particularly Mum. Shadow had been an integral part of Mum's healing journey working through Post Traumatic Stress Disorder, anxiety, and depression. Mum said she was devastated and lost without her. She shared that Shadow had visited her afterwards in a dream and how comforting this was.

I spoke with Shadow and she was very conscious of the trauma Mum was experiencing since her unexpected departure. She said that she was coming back as a blue Chinchilla cat and encouraged Mum to be on the lookout for her. She said Mum would recognise her energy. Shadow's energy was very powerful and it was very moving to have a conversation with her.

Mum was incredibly grateful for these messages and although she had tears, she said it meant so much. She said she never thought she would grieve an animal like this.

I explained to Mum that it means so much to the animals in spirit to be able to get messages to their human and it provides so much reassurance to the human. I've felt my cats in dreams and meditations too and it's their way of comforting you because they know just how much you want to hold them again.

Unfortunately Mum and Shadow did not reconnect as planned – I'm not sure what happened with the Chinchilla cat body that Shadow was planning to reincarnate in.

Some time later Mum reported some strange happenings. The neighbour's cat Daisy who had kept her distance while Shadow was alive had started coming over and was squawking at the back door to come in, something which she'd never done before. Mum was torn between letting her in and leaving her outside since she wasn't her cat. Daisy wasn't going to take no for an answer so finally she was allowed in and made herself at home.

She would sit in Shadow's favourite places and look at Mum in a knowing way. It was intriguing behaviour so I had to find out what was going on. Shadow said she was swapping temporarily into Daisy's body so that she could connect physically with her Mum and have cuddles.

I was aware of animal soul reincarnation but had not experienced temporary animal soul swapping or 'soul overlaying.' The animal soul in spirit negotiates with the soul in the living animal to arrange a brief swap so that the soul in spirit can visit their human in a physical body for a short while. I've since had other experiences with this phenomenon but Shadow and Daisy were the first to help me understand this concept and how it was helping Mum.

CHAPTER 9: Soul secrets

Mum told me that this made so much sense. "Daisy literally hung out with me all day today and was displaying a lot of Shadow's traits. This confirms what I've suspected for a while now." She acknowledged that her connection with Shadow is amazing.

I then was told about another unusual occurrence. Mum told me that Daisy was visiting and curled up on the floor behind her and she could hear a strange noise. When she worked out what was happening, she said she could hear what can only be described as purring coming through her computer speakers! She felt it was Shadow. She said, "It feels weird but cool at the same time." She also shared that Daisy looked straight at her a couple of days ago and she just KNEW Shadow was looking at her through Daisy's eyes. She said she talks to both of them all the time.

I told Mum that I was so glad that Shadow is able to connect with her and spend time with her. I felt that Shadow would be happy knowing that Mum knows she is there. I believe that Shadow has been visiting Mum through Daisy since they weren't able to find each other with the planned reincarnation process. I understood that Shadow wanted to maintain her physical connection with Mum. I also think that the visits will be easing off as Shadow is getting ready to come back and be with Mum in her own new body. She won't need to keep swapping with Daisy. Mum is every confident that Shadow will find a way to come back.

I think the interim solution to connecting with Mum by visiting through Daisy is remarkable. The swapping means she and Mum can experience physical connection through touch, and Mum can receive healing by being able to cuddle and spend time with her. Shadow is reassuring Mum that her soul endures and her love for Mum endures. I think Daisy is so compassionate and accommodating for supporting Shadow to be able to reconnect with Mum in this way. There is no denying the love that animals have for you and their commitment to your wellbeing.

Rocco and Maggie's story

Maggie

Rocco (in spirit) has arranged with his living dog sister Maggie to swap into her body for a brief period of time so he can connect with his Mum. Mum said it is really amazing as Maggie doesn't bark. Since Rocco passed, Maggie will come and sit in front of her in the afternoon, look into her eyes intently and bark at her. Mum sees Maggie's face changing as though she is shapeshifting into

Rocco. When the visit is over, Rocco's soul leaves and Maggie's soul swaps back and everything goes back to normal. Rocco told me that Maggie is a good sport for allowing him to do this.

It's lovely that your animals are so creative and find ways to connect with you, assure you that they are okay, and confirm the enduring nature of your bond.

I've recently spoken with a Mum who is geographically separated from her cat at present. She described a couple of instances where her cat's soul has swapped into her best friend's dog's body. She actually commented, "Why is the dog behaving like the cat?" and then worked out what was happening. This is a case of two living souls temporarily swapping to enable a visit with Mum. It's truly astounding that animals can do this to help us.

CHAPTER 10

Issues with Reconnecting

CHAPTER 10
Issues with Reconnecting

For a variety of reasons, sometimes parents don't actively look for their animals who have provided them with detailed information about their impending reincarnation. They may have moved to temporary accommodation where they are unable to have pets. Their personal situation may have changed. They may not be emotionally ready to renew their relationship. Animals don't judge us. They want to come back just as much as we want them to come back but understand that they may have to wait.

I spoke with one Mum who was reluctant to look for her cat as she was concerned she would fall in love with too many kittens and want to bring them all home! She decided he would have to find his way back to her, and he did!

Parents are also concerned about finding the right animal with their former animal's soul. Some are worried they may choose the wrong animal and that their reincarnated animal may go to a different home. I offer to check the photos of the new animal that people have found and can clarify if the soul of their former animal has swapped in yet, or if not, if that is the body that their soul will definitely be swapping into. So many parents who have been searching for their reincarnated animal have been successfully reunited with them and know beyond a doubt that it's their former animal's soul in their new animal.

In cases where the soul has negotiated to swap into a body and for some reason they are unable to complete the swap, animals search for another option so that they can return to their family. Sometimes an owner or breeder may decide to keep an animal after initially advertising it. Sometimes the animal may have significant health issues or pass away. Whatever the circumstances, your animal's soul wants you to know and trust that they will find a way home. Sometimes they manage to find another body matching the details they provided, and sometimes they have to go to Plan B and come back in a different body than they had originally described and negotiated, but they do come back.

CHAPTER 11

Multiple Dimensionality and Simultaneous Lifetimes

CHAPTER 11
Multiple Dimensionality and Simultaneous Lifetimes

Traditionally humans understand that time is linear. We have the past, we exist in the present and we anticipate the future.

On a soul level, reality is quite different. Time is not linear. Multiple aspects of any soul can be incarnate at the same time in multiple lifetimes. There can be an aspect of your soul now existing in many lifetimes simultaneously.

Through experiences of talking with animals in spirit and their reincarnated versions, animals have explained that there is an aspect of the soul that stays in heaven and that a higher evolved aspect of the soul reincarnates. I wondered why there is an aspect that stays on the other side. I was told that this is the soul anchor. This is the continuous connection for the other aspects of soul existing in different time periods at the same time. Animals have described this phenomenon as soul symbiosis – multiple aspects of the soul existing at the same time in different locations and different time periods but all being energetically inseparable components of the entire soul.

As I am so curious about soul journeys, I have personally experienced past life regressions during light hypnosis and visited lifetimes going back more than 10,000 years. I've also experienced future lifetimes. I've experienced flashbacks to past lives when I've been at significant locations. I understand that you see what your soul wants you to see. As a human I have no conscious remembrance

CHAPTER 11: Multiple dimensionality and simultaneous lifetimes

of my past lives (human or animal) and no conscious awareness that there may be several versions of me currently in existence.

Animals are different from humans. They can recall their past lives in this dimension. They also travel between energetic dimensions. They are here physically with us now transitioning to the 5th dimension, but some of them are also travelling to or working in higher dimensions up to the 12th dimension.

Energetically animals can adjust their light bodies (energetic bodies) more easily to higher dimensions and can evolve and ascend on a spiritual path at an accelerated pace. It also means that animals can more easily hold higher frequencies and understand so much more about universal truths and reality.

When the soul aspect ends a lifetime, it is reunited with the other soul aspects in heaven. All of the aspects together upgrade and align frequency to the highest level in the collective. The soul aspects not in heaven can communicate with each other through an energy network. This capacity underpins their understanding of different lifetimes. Their ability to articulate details from other lives is astonishing.

On accomplishing the soul's purpose, the soul aspects can finally all reunite simultaneously. This is the universal completion of soul ascension. These souls can continue to visit Earth energetically but no longer need to reincarnate as they in combination have mastered all of their soul lessons.

CHAPTER 12

Dying to Come Back

CHAPTER 12
Dying to Come Back

Animals have acknowledged that sometimes they transition earlier than you'd like so that they can come back. It's not the end of a lifetime. It's the end of a chapter of their life and time for reflection and preparation for the next chapter when it aligns with their soul purpose to return. It seems some animal souls have committed to being with us in multiple lifetimes to support our life purpose – a soul contract to keep connecting and evolving together.

Animals have such strong heart connections with their humans that they want to reincarnate as soon as they can to limit the physical separation. They have now let me understand that sometimes they do depart earlier than we expect because the opportunity to reincarnate has been brought forward. Sometimes the body to swap into becomes available earlier than negotiated. It means that our animals can reincarnate earlier but when we don't know what's happening we can be shocked by their sudden departure.

Animals appear to have successive lifetimes closer together than humans do, and many have several lifetimes with their humans.

CHAPTER 12: Dying to come back

Rocco's story

Rocco

Rocco's Mum contacted me after searching for an animal medium who could connect her with her beloved boy dog in spirit, to assist with her grief. She had questions for Rocco, and for his living fur sister dog Maggie.

One of the questions Mum wanted me to ask Rocco was "who is he with on the other side?" From experience, this is a tricky question to ask. Sometimes our animals have struck up new friendships with animals and humans in heaven so do not mention the animals and humans in spirit that their parents are expecting them to mention, and the parents may be disappointed.

When I asked Rocco who he was with, he said, "Charlie and Dusty." I asked if they were humans or animals and he answered, "Four footers," so I assumed that they were animals. I checked several times for confirmation of the names as I wanted to pass on correct information to Mum. He didn't share any further information about them.

He then told me that he is going to reincarnate in his Mum's lifetime, and described exactly what he will look like when he comes back. He also asked for his Mum to consider the name 'Rusty' for him.

After answering the rest of Mum's questions he said the word "treehouse." He didn't explain what it meant, so I assumed this was his "code word" for his Mum to confirm for her that I was definitely speaking with him. I had no idea of the meaning and relevance of a dog telling me "treehouse." I couldn't visualise a dog climbing up little steps to a treehouse so I included it in the conversation transcript for Mum and looked forward to hearing her explanation of the significance.

I was concerned about giving Mum the correct names of who Rocco is spending time with on the other side. When I started the conversation with Maggie she spontaneously told me, "Mum will know who Charlie is, and Dusty is Duke." Maggie obviously knew I needed confirmation that the names Rocco had provided me with were correct. I had no idea who Duke was, but included this in the conversation report too. I also had no idea that Maggie had been eavesdropping on my conversation with Rocco!

Maggie answered her questions and I typed up the transcript of both conversations and emailed the report to Mum. I sent her a message to say that the report had been emailed. She was eager to know how her boy was, and I asked her to read the report.

CHAPTER 12: Dying to come back

A few minutes later, I received a message saying "Holy #$*%. He's with Charlie and Dusty. There's no way you could have known that! I'm completely blown away!"

We had a debrief Zoom chat the following day to go through the animals' responses and for Mum to explain the significance of what her dogs had shared with me. She told me that Dusty was her first dog when she was about 3 years old and she absolutely loved the dog. Sadly they had to move and couldn't take the dog so she was heartbroken and the dog was left with a neighbour. Duke was her next dog when she was about 8. Mum is very intuitive and had felt when she got Rocco that he had Duke's soul. With Rocco reincarnating as the puppy Rusty, this will be the 4th time his soul has been connected with his Mum in this lifetime. It's no coincidence he mentioned the name 'Rusty' as a combination of Rocco and Dusty – he was sending a message confirming who he is with the various reincarnations. Now Mum knows Rocco's soul is linked with Dusty and Duke. I know several people who have recognised aspects of the same soul in three successive animals, but Rocco will be the first I know to have four successive lifetimes in one human's lifetime when he returns as a puppy.

Charlie is Mum's cousin's dog in spirit. He and Rocco spent a lot of time together when alive even though they weren't particularly close, but because their human Mums spent time together. Interestingly Mum and her cousin have joked about the boys probably spending time together on the other side, and they are!

Mum explained that Treehouse is a property she has visited numerous times with Rocco. Opposite the property there are lots of walking tracks where Rocco has walked with his Mum from puppyhood till just before he passed away. This was a really meaningful code word for Rocco to have chosen for his Mum evoking memories of happy times together.

Mum said, "You've helped me in ways you could never imagine."

This is one of the reasons why I do what I do – I love being able to support bereaved animal parents by connecting with the soul of their animal in spirit and confirming that they have transitioned safely and that their soul endures. It can really help the grief process knowing that your animal is okay, and that they are contactable no matter how long ago they passed. Having a conversation can help achieve peace of mind for you and for them.

Since our conversation, both Mum and I have randomly seen the words Dusty and Rusty in unusual places – in word puzzles, embroidered on a hat, the name of a restaurant, and on a piece of paper that landed in an animal memorial garden.

Rocco is continuing to send signs confirming that he is returning soon.

Gemmah's story

Gemmah

CHAPTER 12: Dying to come back

Mum had owned and worked with a number of horses doing dressage, and competing in events. She said Gemmah's arrival was momentous, and different from any other relationship with a horse.

She wasn't actively looking for a horse yet was often at a stable with her friend who had a horse stabled there. A veterinarian who wondered why she didn't have a horse asked if she was looking for one and she replied, "Not really, because of the expense." He said he knew where two were for sale and encouraged her to go and look at them advising that they would be inexpensive to purchase. If they didn't sell they were going to be put down.

Mum was really drawn to the horse she named 'Gemmah', but she didn't know why she felt so strongly about her. She went and spent time with Gemmah in her stall connecting with her energetically. She felt instinctively that Gemmah would help her to compete in higher level dressage events than she had currently achieved. She felt a strong connection and gentleness with Gemmah, and was successful with her purchase offer.

She initially halter-trained Gemmah, but their intuitive bond developed to such a level that Gemmah understood innately what Mum wanted her to do and no longer needed the halter. People were amazed watching them work together with no verbal instructions.

When Gemmah was originally boarded till Mum was able to take her home, she would come running when Mum called her. Once Gemmah was on Mum's property, Mum would send her telepathic messages. Mum said Gemmah used to nicker in advance when Mum was physically approaching the stables, sensing Mum's energetic frequency.

Gemmah's sire was an Olympic Champion show jumper, so she had pedigree genes to succeed. In their first dressage show, Gemmah and Mum won both events they'd competed in. Gemmah went on to win numerous dressage and jumping events during her lifetime.

Mum ended up having to sell Gemmah when she was moving, which was really difficult given their relationship. Her incredible bond with Gemmah continued even though they were physically separated. Many years later Gemmah came to visit Mum in a dream. Mum found out the next day that Gemmah had passed away. Such a remarkable life of achievement and love for a horse that the original owner rejected. It was beautiful of Gemmah to visit Mum on her last day acknowledging their incredible connection.

Some years later Mum and her daughter were at the Humane Society. Her daughter's cat had passed away and they were ready to welcome another cat into the family. The daughter wandered off to see who was available. Mum idly looked in a cage, and a female cat was staring directly at her. Mum liked the look of the cat, even though she wasn't looking for one. A staff member commented that the cat was looking at her. The staff member was about to clean the cat's enclosure and asked Mum if she'd like to spend time with her. Mum picked up the cat and sat with her. The staff member said no one had been able to pick her up. Mum and her daughter took two cats home! Mum said she couldn't have left the cat there.

Mum's cat was christened 'Abbi'. She needed lots of love and reassurance to desensitise her after whatever trauma she had experienced prior to arriving at the rescue agency. Mum started training Abbi to do agility routines on the sofa. Abbi would

CHAPTER 12: Dying to come back

run across the room and land exactly where Mum wanted her to, reading her mind like Gemmah did. It was another similar relationship with telepathic communication and a soul connection. Mum knows that Abbi chose her, and recognises that Gemmah's soul aspect was in Abbi. There was no denying the similar energetic connection and intuitive understanding. Mum knew the connection between them was special. She also saw the similarity of Abbi learning and remembering the precision of training as Gemmah did. The connection of souls is timeless. Observing how souls keep connecting and reconnecting through lifetimes and feeling that magnetic pull and sense of knowing being in their presence defies logic, but it's real.

After Abbi passed away, Mum used to visit a friend who had a lot of cats. She lived on a large property and looked after any cat in need. Mum noticed that one of the barn cats called 'Ava' would always know when she was visiting. It didn't matter what day or time – when Mum was at the gate Ava would appear. She was tuned in energetically and intuitively to Mum. She didn't exhibit this behaviour with any other visitors. I went buzzy listening to this story. Abbi had found a way to reconnect with her human. Their intuitive connection and understanding of each other is incredible. It's so astonishing that the soul aspect in Gemmah, Abbi and Ava has been able to have multiple lifetimes with Mum, support her, and change her life in such profound ways.

Toby's story

Toby (L) & Cindy

Dad shared his story describing it as "coincidences that defy explanation."

Toby was his loved 100 kg plus German Shepherd Rottweiler mix dog who was very protective of the whole family and property. He and his sister dog Cindy guarded the yard which periodically was invaded by cobras. Sadly Cindy had a heart problem and passed away after a cobra bite. Toby was deeply affected by his sister's passing. He too succumbed to a cobra attack and went to be reunited with his sister on the other side.

A while later Dad welcomed a female calf called Sandy. Dad didn't think anything of it at the time, but Sandy would sleep in the same places that Toby did, including under the water tower. Sandy then progressed to sleeping in the garden where Cindy and Toby are buried.

Cindy and Toby used to run to the garden gate to wait for Dad's granddaughter to come home from school. Sandy now runs to the

CHAPTER 12: Dying to come back

gate and the granddaughter rides her to the front door. The dogs loved being hugged strongly with Dad's arms around their necks. Sandy is the same, and nudges Dad for a hug. Sandy runs up to Dad like a dog.

The dogs used to wait till each had a food bowl served before eating. Sandy (now grown up) and her calf Mandy do exactly the same thing when they are fed.

Cindy, Toby and now Sandy all have a liking for strawberry ice cream.

This is such an incredible story. The dogs never met Sandy. How does Sandy know where Toby slept and where his grave is? How does Sandy know to do the afternoon pickup with the granddaughter? Why does she love being hugged and how does she know to signal that she wants a hug? Why does she run like a dog? Why does she exhibit the dogs' eating behaviour?

Most animals tend to reincarnate as the same species, but perhaps a different breed. Sandy is an exception to this. I went buzzy when I heard this story for the first time, which was confirmation for me that Toby's soul had reincarnated in Sandy. A dog came back as a cow. It sounds bizarre, but there are so many similarities.

Key learnings:

- Your animals, if they do reincarnate, don't necessarily come back as the same species.

- If you notice something familiar about your new animal, be open to the fact that you may have the soul of a previous animal with you.

- I encourage people to thank their animal by their original name for coming back, so that they know you know who they are. Often they can be quite vocal trying to let you know who they are, and it's such a relief when you finally understand. They can then relax and enjoy having their next lifetime with you, resuming and deepening your original relationship.

KitKat's story

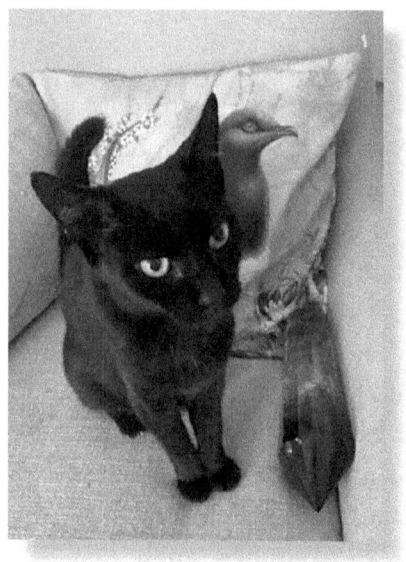

KitKat

I had the fortune of connecting with the gorgeous black cat KitKat while she was alive. She had some significant health issues and was also working on an energetic level to support her humans. She was an evolved soul and very wise. She loved the frequency of crystals.

After her passing, Mum asked me to connect with her to find out if she had messages or wisdom to share. KitKat provided lots of

CHAPTER 12: Dying to come back

spiritual advice and practical advice to assist her humans. She asked that her funeral urn be kept in the corridor so she could continue providing protection.

She then told me that she was going to reincarnate as a ginger male cat. She was totally unimpressed about having to come back as a male – she really wanted to be a female again. She told me Mum would find her by the end of September that year. She said she wanted to be called 'Hugo Boss.' She loved being the boss of the family and was preparing them for her undertaking a similar role.

Mum searched everywhere for a ginger male kitten with no luck. On the last day of September she saw a car number plate that reminded her of her cousin. She contacted her cousin, who unbeknownst to Mum happened to have a litter of ginger kittens who had been born two days earlier! Mum brought home the male ginger kitten and his sister kitten who she named 'Harriet.'

Hugo

KitKat as Hugo had to adjust to being a male and being in a new body. Hugo was not expecting to have to share the limelight and his humans with his sister. It took a while for both cats to accept that they were going to be living together and that they needed to sort things out. They have done this and now get on amicably.

Hugo has continued being very protective of his Mum and loves spending time with Mum's crystals.

Key wisdom:

- Animals are so willing to assist you, and they love being asked for messages and guidance to help their humans. They are very intuitive and insightful and what they tell you may be very profound and powerful to help you progress with your spiritual evolvement.

- Although there seems to be some choice with the breed animals reincarnate as, often the gender may not be their preference. I've had conversations with a number of animals who came back as a different gender. Although they may not be thrilled with this, the overriding factor is that they get to return to their humans and their concerns about their gender then fade into insignificance.

- Some of your animals are here with a special role as healers and will deliberately be living and working with humans who are healers. Some may have had past lives as human healers. Some of these animals are very experienced with healing modalities from previous lifetimes, and it's so interesting seeing their affinity with crystals. They can sense the energetic frequencies and understand the healing potential.

CHAPTER 12: Dying to come back

Marley's story

Charlie and Coco – a love story

Marley

Mum won a conversation with me and used it to connect with her beautiful dog Marley who had been diagnosed with a terminal condition. He and Mum had an incredibly close bond and Mum was doing everything she could to maintain his quality of life for as long as he wanted to stay.

She was considering getting a female puppy but didn't want to cause stress for Marley. She wanted to respect his energy reserves and not overwhelm him. She wanted to know if he could cope with a female puppy. He said, "Yes" and told us he would have a second puppyhood with her. He also said how glad he was that Mum would have someone to hold and love when it was his time to pass over.

He said he was going to stay as long as he could as he adored his Mum and that she would recognise particular changes in him when it was his time to leave.

Mum welcomed the female puppy Coco into the family and she and Marley developed a close relationship. I had the privilege of talking with Marley on the day he passed away and was able to convey messages from his Mum to him and his goodbye to his Mum. He showed me an image of wings so I thought he must have passed, then Mum sent me a photo of him with wings on his back that she'd placed there. It's a beautiful photo taken just before his soul transitioned. He told his Mum that he would come back for energetic visits and she would feel his tail wagging against her.

After Marley left, Coco really supported her Mum and helped her through the grief process. Marley had known that his Mum would need this assistance to help adjusting to his absence.

During my next conversation with Marley in spirit he told us that he was coming back as the same breed with the same colours and would be a male again.

Charlie (L) and Coco

CHAPTER 12: Dying to come back

It was so wonderful to be sent the photo of the puppy Mum found and confirm that Marley's soul was in the puppy. Marley is now 'Charlie' and looks and acts so much the same that he often gets called Marley. He and Coco renewed their relationship and have now produced three litters of beautiful puppies. Charlie didn't get the chance to be a father as Marley so he has embraced the new experiences and responsibilities. He has excelled sharing the raising of the puppies and has also taken care of kittens. The bond he has with Coco is incredible and there is more to their story.

Mum also asked me to have a conversation with her soul dog Lily in spirit. Lily was a beautiful dog both with her appearance and in her nature. Mum shared her wedding photos which Lily featured in and I could feel their strong connection.

Lily

Lily had endured some significant health issues and Mum had questions about the advice she received and decisions made at the end of Lily's life. Lily was able to answer Mum's medical questions and ease Mum's ongoing concerns and emotions surrounding her passing.

Mum is very intuitive and had a feeling that Lily had reincarnated as Coco. Lily confirmed this and said, "I'm glad you've worked that out." Even though Mum experienced deep grief with her passing, Lily said, "It's definitely wonderful to be back. I'm happy and healthy, so please let go of the past – your Lily is with you. Our deep love connection persists."

Lily also explained that she and Charlie are soulmates, so they both had to come back to be together again.

Seeing the photos of Charlie and Coco together and with their puppies is so beautiful and moving, especially knowing the soul connections with Marley, Lily, and Mum. Charlie and Coco share such a deep love and it's truly remarkable that they are now back in healthy bodies to renew and evolve their soulmate relationship.

Key wisdom:

- Animals understand we go through a grief process when we say goodbye. They understand that having another animal can greatly assist us with our grief.

- Sometimes our reincarnated animals look and behave very similarly to their previous lifetime.

- It's so reassuring that animals in spirit can return for energetic visits. Marley was specific with knowing Mum was going to be

CHAPTER 12: Dying to come back

able to feel the sensation of his tail wagging. It is very surreal to see, hear or feel your animal's presence when they come for a visit. Your other animals will also benefit from these visits as it will help to ease their grief too.

- Since our animals have a good understanding of medical conditions, they can explain their health issues.

Babe's story

Babe

Babe's Mum was given an animal mediumship conversation with me as a gift. She was eager to connect with her beautiful and beloved Dobermann girl in spirit and receive the answers to her questions.

Mum asked if she was happy, and Babe said she was, running and jumping and so many trees. She didn't explain what the significance of the trees was so I asked Mum to interpret that message. Mum explained that she and Babe did a lot of travelling and they would run and jump amongst the trees. Babe loved playing hide and seek in the trees and chasing her Mum. She was so relieved to hear this response which also confirmed her safe transition.

There were also questions about other dogs and about Mum's new Chihuahua Pablo. Babe admitted that she was involved in Pablo coming to Mum to help heal her heart. She said Pablo had a lot of love to give and that he was committed and dedicated to Mum. Babe said that she and Pablo chat a lot about Mum. Pablo said he was very content with the love he was receiving.

Mum said to pass on how much she loves Babe and that she misses her every day. Babe knew how sad her Mum was, that Pablo was there to help fill some of the void, and that her love for Mum is unwavering. She described a trinket and a toy teddy and said that she was happy for Pablo to have these. Mum confirmed that she had saved the trinket and Babe's favourite teddy. Apparently Babe was happy to share her older teddies with other dogs but was very protective of her new ones.

Babe appreciated having the conversation and I told her I'd send the conversation report which she had requested to Mum on Mum's birthday. Babe also told me, "Words can't say how much I love her."

I told Mum that I hoped that the conversation would ease her mind and heart.

CHAPTER 12: Dying to come back

Mum thanked me from her heart. She said Babe gave her enormous peace about some of her concerns. She told me that the conversation with Babe showed her that the connection she felt they had built in that last two years of her life was not a figment of her imagination. She said it was real and true and as special as she felt it was. She told me that Pablo became a lot more attentive following the conversation and seemed more relaxed. She wasn't sure how she could love anyone else after Babe, but Pablo has claimed a part of her heart.

Pablo

When Mum sent me her thank you email, she included a photo of Pablo who I hadn't seen before. When I saw the photo of Pablo I cried - happy tears. It was a question I hadn't asked Babe but with having such a strong reaction to the photo I chatted with her again to confirm my thoughts about her connection with Pablo.

Babe said she knew I would figure it out, and that's why she mentioned the trinket and teddy. It's an aspect of her soul in Pablo. Babe came back to be with her Mum!

I wondered how Mum would respond to this momentous news.

Mum said it was confirmation of the ONE question which was most important to her which she chose not to ask. She intuitively knew who Pablo was but needed more practice trusting her intuition. She knew that if she was right that I would answer her question without her asking it.

She said, "Thank you is not remotely sufficient for the gift you have just given me."

Key learnings:

- Many animal parents have reported a deeper and more affectionate relationship with their animal after having a conversation. They know that you know their answers. It confirms for them that you care so much that you wanted the conversation to happen and have questions answered.

- For animals in spirit, having a mediumship conversation with them is the first opportunity since they passed over to really connect with you and pass on messages of love, gratitude, and guidance.

- Intuition is a gift that we all have and we can develop it. It takes faith and time to trust our intuition and be guided by the messages we receive. It is a powerful tool to help us navigate life.

- Having a soul aspect of our animals reincarnate and come back to us is such a miraculous occurrence and there is such an overflowing of joy when animals and humans reunite.

CHAPTER 12: Dying to come back

Many animal parents are not aware that their animal has reincarnated and it totally changes the interactions when you realise who they are.

A lot of animal parents have rued the fact that animals have such relatively short lives with us. Animals are more pragmatic about this. They know that they can come back and keep coming back.

Moonlight's story

Barford   Moonlight

Having an extremely close soul connection with your cat for over 19 years is an amazing experience and when my client's beloved cat Barford passed away the loss was significant.

After some time, Mum adopted a rescue cat she called 'Moonlight' who looked different to Barford but had similar stunning yellow topaz coloured eyes. He was vocally very chatty and Mum wanted to know what he was trying to tell her. When we had a conversation he revealed that he had Barford's soul and that he had come back to be with his human. I spoke with Barford and he confirmed that his soul had reincarnated. He said, "He is me and I am he." He commented how wonderful it was to be home, and conveyed the depth of his love for his Mum. Moonlight was so relieved that his Mum finally knew who he was and they continued their close and loving relationship.

I was shocked when Mum contacted me some months later to say that Moonlight had unexpectedly passed away. He was such an affectionate cat and so thrilled to be back with his Mum but tragically he passed earlier than any of us had anticipated, including him. When I connected with him he was just as shocked with his sudden departure but wanted some time to find another body so that he could return to his Mum as soon as possible.

When I spoke with him a few days later as he had requested, he had found a cat body to swap into. He told me that he was at a particular animal rescue organisation which was a few hours' drive from his Mum and that he was female! I looked online at the available female cats and found a beautiful girl who wasn't very old with a lot of white fur like Moonlight and with striking yellow eyes. I just wanted to cry looking at her so my soul recognised that this was the new higher evolved version of Barford and Moonlight. It was such a relief to know that Moonlight had found a way to get back to his Mum so quickly. It was so exciting to update Mum about this. She had been devastated with losing Moonlight but now had hope with him returning.

Mum had to contact the organisation and express interest in the kitten and be considered as her adopter. Unfortunately the kitten had a health issue similar to what Barford had experienced when he was young so she was considered 'not available' for adoption till

CHAPTER 12: Dying to come back

the vets were satisfied with her health status. It's so interesting to observe the parallels in different lifetimes.

Luna

I received a message early one morning from Mum advising that the kitten, who she has christened 'Luna', had recovered and was now ready and approved for adoption. Mum collected Luna and she has settled back into her familiar home quickly. Mum says she is very affectionate and following her everywhere. She is already exhibiting some of Moonlight's behaviours and postures confirming who she is.

Key wisdom:

- It is one of the highlights of my work hearing about the reunions and receiving the photos and knowing the healing that will occur for both animal and human being back together again.

- The experience with Moonlight taught me so much. He was my first reincarnated client to pass away and like his Mum I thought his passing would be years away. I was impressed with his determination to get back to his Mum as soon as he could. He was extremely specific with the location where Mum would find him. Negotiating to swap with the rescue kitten happened within 48 hours of our conversation. Waiting for the health issue to resolve delayed the homecoming, but it was definitely worth it to welcome this beautiful girl with the soulful eyes and a heart filled with love. Sometimes there are unexpected hiccoughs with the reincarnation process but the animals are absolutely committed to finding a solution and being reunited with their humans.

Pixie's story

Pixie

CHAPTER 12: Dying to come back

Pixie is a beautiful cat in spirit who was very precise with the details answering her Mum's questions, and totally aware of what was happening with her and her Mum.

When asked if and when she was reincarnating, she said she would be in her new body in seven weeks. She said, "I'll be a red/orange (ginger) domestic short hair boy cat with white socks and less than 3 months old. He's pretty cute so I don't mind being a boy." She said her soul hadn't swapped into him yet. She advised Mum that it might take her 3-4 weeks before she found the right kitten online.

Mum was curious to find out if Pixie would continue to have a guide role with her or if she would reincarnate with a completely different purpose. Pixie reassured Mum saying, "I'm always available to guide her – that was my purpose being with her. When I reincarnate, the part of me who comes back will have a different purpose but I will definitely be there to support her too."

Since Pixie had been her guide, Mum wanted to know if she had any specific advice for her before she returned. Pixie provided this comprehensive reply: "You have to learn to trust and listen to your own intuition and guidance. It's developing but you just don't trust it yet. You hold great wisdom and need to share it. It's part of your purpose to speak your truth and help others. You have a big heart – your love is so powerful and I'm so grateful to have been a beneficiary of your love for so long. Be confident that you can do what you put your mind to – you are capable of so much and just need to overcome the blocks to your success that you are creating."

Pixie also revealed that they had shared a past life, that there was a deep bond of affection between them and that she was counting down the days until she was back.

Mum contacted me recently to update me. She had found the ginger kitten as described within the timeframe as foretold by Pixie. 'Peter' has arrived home and is very contented and has the run of the house. Mum said she whispered 'Pixie' in his ear and he stared straight into her eyes. He is sleeping where Pixie slept. Mum said, "I already feel a very strong bond with him and love him dearly. He is so sweet and mischievous just like Pixie was as a kitten. I am so grateful to you for guiding us back to each other."

Peter

CHAPTER 13

Reality Revealed

CHAPTER 13
Reality Revealed

I am genuinely in awe of what animals know and how much they can help you make sense of reality, your purpose and spiritual growth. The following is what they have told me and what they want you to know.

As souls, you experience multiple cycles of energetic upgrades or ascension activations. These are enhanced by loss, learning and lunar cycles. Sometimes you need to be in a state of turmoil so that your conscious mind is otherwise occupied allowing new information to be absorbed and processed. Two days before Reilly unexpectedly passed away I was hit by a car on a pedestrian crossing. It jolted me on an energetic level and Reilly knew I was in a state of shock and energetic flux. She knew that this was the best time for her to transition while I was in a different state of mind. I've just had a conversation with Molly, a dog in spirit, who knew her unexpected departure would trigger accelerated awakening and growth for her human family so that with her return (reincarnation) they can resume work together at a more advanced spiritual level.

The conscious mind can block soul evolvement. Thinking rationally and logically can inhibit receptivity to foreign and seemingly bizarre concepts and energetic downloads. Animals learn, integrate, and evolve at a faster pace, embracing and accepting the new and previously hidden facts and explanations of reality with ease. My cats are transmitting all of this information to me

CHAPTER 13: Reality revealed

effortlessly – they comprehend what you don't know and what you need to understand to help you progress on your spiritual journey.

As many animals are highly evolved souls who have experienced multiple lifetimes as humans and animals, they have a huge wealth of knowledge to share. They are adept teachers and guides for you when you are ready to listen. They are wise, they are patient and they want you to succeed and realise the limitless potential in the reality of life.

This is a critical concept for you: living life guided by a new paradigm whereby you understand reality with a deeper, more encompassing and enlightened focus exponentially affects and enables your consciousness expansion.

Another key learning that animals want you to recognise is your connection with Source (God), nature and each other. Everything living consists of energy and vibrational frequency and everything living is connected. There is indeed a living consciousness of interconnectedness even though you don't understand that you can consciously connect. So many people don't understand yet that you can communicate with animals and have profound conversations that change your lives.

Your thoughts and the words you utter have vibrational frequency and ripple out and affect every soul in your energetic field and beyond. Animals are definitely aware of your energetic field and any changes. What you say to your animals and how you say it affects them. There is research showing that talking to plants has beneficial effects including improved growth and improved resistance to disease. Like animals, plants are sensitive to the vibrations of words and respond to them. Vibrational frequencies connect all living things.

Some of you experience temporary disconnection from Source/ God. When you find your way back you can reconnect with the higher consciousness where you know innately that there is so much more to life than your daily routines. My cats escorted me in a meditation to feel the pure energy of God. It was an almost overwhelming sensation of high frequency powerful love, security and tenderness enveloping me. I was shown unending gold and pink colour frequencies denoting the Divine and eternal love. Your animals can help you interpret Divine guidance – they can act as messengers and they know what you are supposed to be doing during your life journey.

There are oceans of love surrounding you. You can always access this infinite love. Animals help you by radiating their love. For some people, having an animal is their only opportunity to experience love, both receiving and giving. Animals love you unconditionally – there are no terms. We are their humans and their love for us is constant throughout their life and in the afterlife. Since their souls are eternal, your connections with them are eternal. The bond of love transcends all dimensions of time and space, including your past, present, parallel and future lives being lived simultaneously. You recognise the power of that bond when they reincarnate. Love never dies.

Your animals are so much more than 'pets.' Some of them have unique knowledge and skill sets to help with your life mission. They help you to comprehend the mysteries of reality.

CHAPTER 13: Reality revealed

Animals and humans may both have had human or animal lifetimes previously

We exist as souls in animal or human bodies. We are each forms of intelligence and we can learn from each other. Earth is like a giant Mystery School from the ancient civilizations with so many concepts to hear, see, experience and understand.

There is so much wisdom to tap into which will really help you. Animals are guides who have travelled through time deliberately to help you at this time.

"Although it may seem impossible to you, we are here to help. What we collectively know surpasses your understanding. Teaching is what we are here to do when you are on the same wavelength and can hear and interpret our transmissions. We understand all languages so can communicate with all. Traditionally we have been called 'dumb animals' but that is far from the truth. We are here to challenge those assumptions and limitations and help you understand far greater wisdom than you could ever imagine."

The world is going through phenomenal change on so many levels and much does not make sense. There is a greater purpose and people will understand more as their vibrational frequency rises. "Part of our purpose is to support that ascension process to help humans evolve. We have done this teaching for time immemorial. We have a great capacity to store and recall knowledge and to impart it so that it can activate and expand your consciousness. It is our purpose to help yours. We love being of service and witnessing your progress."

"Before now we have been limited in the number of people we can access and impart wisdom to, but that situation is improving as more people wake up and understand animals as intellectual equals. Destiny is sometimes obtuse. You can't see where you are going and sometimes you don't know where you're going, but you have experience and gifts and our support to guide you so that you can fulfil your soul mission. Some of us keep coming back for multiple lifetimes because as souls we have committed to see your journey through."

"You will experience moments of breakthroughs and realisations. The world is not as it seems. There are so many layers of wisdom and knowledge learnt from the past and future which we can apply now. We can reveal information and guidance for you when you can understand how to receive it. We can impart this wisdom in a gentle way to not overwhelm you. We are happy to help explain what seems inexplicable and share what you need to know to progress forward on your soul journeys. You could consider us spiritual emissaries.

Listening to us will fundamentally change your paradigms of thinking and knowledge. There is no scientific explanation or rational or logical or analytical process to explain some of what we know. The truth can seem confronting but it is what it is. In time you can adjust and accept a new way of understanding reality and embrace previously unknown universal truths. We don't want to bombard you as your consciousness expands. We can give you the facts to take your next steps forwards. Some of you may feel stuck or feel lost and not know what direction to take next. Understanding your life mission or spiritual purpose and your soul lessons makes these

CHAPTER 13: Reality revealed

decisions and actions much easier to implement. You can have more certainty about what you need to do."

There is some truth in the saying, "It's not the destination that's important, it's the journey." Yes, where you are going and what you are going to achieve is important, but how you get there and how you evolve as you take the steps to get there is extremely important. Who you were in the past is not going to be who you are in the future. As you evolve spiritually, your vibrational frequency will rise and you will radiate a different frequency which people around you and animals around you will respond to.

As your questions are answered, there will be a myriad more. There is always more to learn and more to remember from the past that you can use now to help yourselves and each other. Animals are here to help you on your life path. Their role is so much more important than most people have given them credit for. It's interesting in the creation story that animals were created before humans and also that the animals could communicate with the humans. Animals have important roles on the planet. Humans can connect with animals and communicate with them and be the beneficiaries of the innate and impressive wisdom that they hold.

Animals can communicate telepathically from a very young age. I have spoken with my cat Tiernay from 6 weeks of age when I first met him energetically. Animals can also have separate conversations at the same time. I had a very profound conversation with a wise white lion who was having multiple conversations with different people about different topics simultaneously. Their communication abilities are advanced.

Animals can help you to put the pieces together understanding how everything is related to everything else. They can broaden your horizons, deepen your comprehension and accelerate your consciousness expansion and soul evolution. Now is the opportune time for you to learn and grow – there are no limits and anything is possible.

Animals exemplify how experience builds on experience with multiple reincarnations. They describe this as metamorphosis of the soul. Learning and applying animal intelligence is a crucial part of your future as humans and evolving souls. There is still so much more to learn and understand, and animals are here to teach you and assist you now and in the future. You can benefit so much from interacting with animals – ultimately fast-tracking your soul growth and achieving higher consciousness.

More wisdom is yet to be revealed.

ACKNOWLEDGEMENTS

Thank you to my cats for their wisdom, intuition, support and healing, and their contributions to this book.

Thank you to all of the animals and their human parents who gave their permission to share their incredible stories of love and connection, and their photographs.

I appreciate every conversation I have with animals. The knowledge they share expands my awareness, enabling me to raise global consciousness about animals, and inherently about life.

Thank you to Sumiko Takesue Eyears from Sumico Photography https://www.sumicophotography.com.au/ for my author profile photo with Tiernay.

Thank you to Zoo Studio https://www.zoostudio.com.au/ for the cover photo of Naoise.

Thank you to Janine from Furry Souls for her care and compassion in providing the beautiful funeral urns my cats requested https://www.petcremationurns.com.au/

Thank you to Rochelle and Jenny for your assistance.

To Jane Goodall, Leonardo DiCaprio and David Attenborough – thank you for the inspirational work you do opening our eyes to the wonder of animals in the wild and the importance of making a difference for them while we still have time.

To Diana Cooper – thank you for sharing your wisdom about the energetic significance and contributions of animals across the dimensions.

CONNECT WITH ANNIE

I'd love to help enrich your relationships with your animals. You can enrol in the telepathic Animal Communication Mentorship Program and talk with your animals living and in spirit. You can also arrange conversations with your animals to have your questions answered.

Please email me at CHIntuitive@bigpond.com so we can have a conversation.

Please connect with me on social media:

Facebook Personal page: https://www.facebook.com/profile.php?id=100011229976148

Facebook Business page: https://www.facebook.com/CosmicHeartIntuitive

LinkedIn Personal page: https://www.linkedin.com/in/anniebourkecosmicheartintuitive/

Visit my website https://www.cosmicheartintuitive.com.au/ and access my free guides for animal parents.

My podcast "What animals tell me" features some of my amazing experiences with animals. You can listen to episodes here: https://podcasters.spotify.com/pod/show/annie6509

Subscribe to my YouTube channel and watch my animal story videos and interviews https://www.youtube.com/channel/UCiWk7nu1K8skogPonW9_nhQ

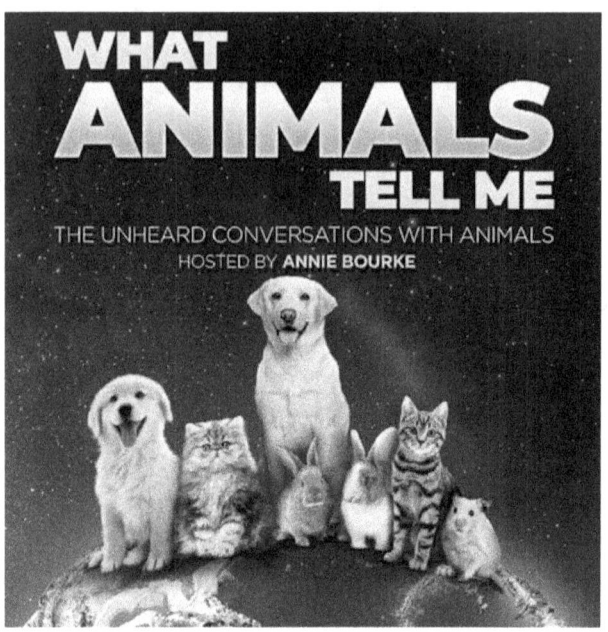

You are invited to join my private Facebook group "Consciously understanding your animals" which is a community of animal parents sharing their animals and experiences as animal parents.

I present and livestream free monthly masterclasses and promote other events in the group. Join me here: https://www.facebook.com/groups/understandingyouranimals

ABOUT ANNIE
Author, Animal Communicator, Animal Medium, Healer and Clairsentient

Annie is an international bestselling author, animal communicator and animal medium, healer and clairsentient. Animals are her passion. She supports both animals and people in her Cosmic Heart Intuitive telepathic sessions having conversations with animals living and in spirit.

An all-round animal lover, Annie has had a lifelong affinity with cats, both large and small. Her passion for all animals started just after she could walk when she snuck outside unsupervised to watch birds. She met and fed kangaroos as a four year old.

Annie has since travelled the world visiting animals in the wild, in sanctuaries and in zoos. From bears in Alaska to emperor penguins in Antarctica, she loves being in the energy of animals and accessing their wisdom! Annie's mission is to raise global awareness of the importance of animals.

Her whole world changed when she began her animal communication training, and she now supports animal parents around the world to telepathically communicate with their pets. These one-on-one mentorship sessions enrich the relationships between animals and their humans.

She has also always been drawn to healing. After having a health professional and business background, Annie had a spiritual awakening and embarked on her pursuit to explore all things metaphysical so she could truly understand the nature of reality. She now helps people with their spiritual awakening and self-development journeys.

Annie has studied the Japanese energy healing method Reiki, as well as crystal therapy, aromatherapy, mediumship and animal communication. She combines natural healing modalities to support animals and their humans.

She has had articles published online and in magazines, spoken at events, and been a guest on numerous international podcasts and summits to talk about her work with animals and how human parents can better connect with and understand their pets. Annie also hosts her own podcast 'What animals tell me'.

Her short-term vision is to expand the number of people who can communicate with their animals. Her longer-term vision is to create a sanctuary for rescue animals where they can be safe and receive healing, and where she can also host retreats for people who want to learn energetic healing and master telepathic communication.

Annie lives in Brisbane, Australia. She is the author of *'The Bridge to Animal Consciousness'* and *'Evolving Hearts and Souls —The Guide to Spiritual Awakening'*.

RESOURCES

A unique opportunity to work with Annie
The Conscious Animal Parent Program

1. The telepathic Animal Communication Mentorship Program - be mentored 1:1 by Annie for 3 months to master communicating with your animals living and in spirit. The program includes foundation videos, workbooks, mentorship sessions recordings and audio resources.

2. Annie's bestselling books "The Bridge to Animal Consciousness" and "Evolving Hearts and Souls -The Guide to Spiritual Awakening" with messages from Annie.

3. Masterclasses - Animal Communication Parts 1 & 2, Being an animal parent - advice from animals, and How do I deepen my connection with my animal ?

4. Spiritual development mentoring session.

Contact Annie at CHIntuitive@bigpond.com for program booking enquiries.

Visit https://www.bridginganimalconsciousness.com

FREE GUIDES

Download your FREE guides for animal parents from Annie's website:

https://www.cosmicheartintuitive.com.au/

PURCHASE ANNIE'S FIRST BOOKS

International bestseller "The Bridge to Animal Consciousness" is the first book in the Bridging Animal Consciousness trilogy.

This was written to raise awareness of the importance of animals, which is Annie's life mission.

This book explains:
- Why animals are here
- The wonder of animal soul journeys including reincarnation
- How to welcome an animal to your family, and dealing with goodbyes
- Enriching the lives of animals
- Practical ways to make a difference for animals

Animals matter. They are wise beings who can help you on your journeys. The more you understand them, the richer your lives are.

Amazon #1 Bestseller "Evolving Hearts and Souls – The Guide to Spiritual Awakening" is Annie's second book aimed to help people on their spiritual awakening and spiritual development journey.

When Annie woke up, she had no idea she was waking up and had no idea about spiritual awakenings or what was happening. She couldn't find anyone to explain the weird things she was experiencing particularly when her clairvoyant gift was activated.

Annie shares some of her personal experiences to demystify some of the strange things that happen on your spiritual journey.

Topics include Spiritual development, Meditation, Souls, The energetic body, Spiritual gifts, Healing and more.

If you have wondered why you are here, why you meet people who you feel you already know, or if you see, hear, feel or know things with no rational explanation, then this book can help you feel more confident and better prepared in navigating your spiritual awakening and spiritual growth journey.

To purchase the paperbacks in Australia, contact Annie at CHIntuitive@bigpond.com

To purchase internationally, please visit your local Amazon store online.

LEARN TO TALK WITH YOUR ANIMALS

Would you love to be able to talk with your animals living or in spirit?

Are you frustrated not knowing what they are trying to tell you?

Are you concerned about behaviour changes or health issues?

Mastering telepathic animal communication means you can ask your animals your questions as they arise, and ease your worries by getting prompt answers.

Your animals are here to support you in so many ways, and offer so much more than helping you to experience unconditional love and providing their comfort and companionship.

Are you curious about past soul connections with your animal?

Do you want to know why they are with you?

Would you love to find out the guidance they want to share with you?

Contact Annie at <u>CHIntuitive@bigpond.com</u> to receive the program PDF and enrolment details.

www.ingramcontent.com/pod-product-compliance
Lightning Source LLC
Chambersburg PA
CBHW052035070526
44584CB00016B/2057